T0068065

AGE DISCRIMINATION: AN EPIDEMIC IN AMERICA

AFFECTING PEOPLE OF ALL AGES

JOHN K. HULETT

authorHOUSE®

AuthorHouse™ LLC
1663 Liberty Drive
Bloomington, IN 47403
www.authorhouse.com
Phone: 1-800-839-8640

Published by AuthorHouse   10/30/2013

ISBN: 978-1-4670-5450-8 (sc)
ISBN: 978-1-4670-5451-5 (hc)
ISBN: 978-1-4670-5452-2 (e)

Library of Congress Control Number: 2011918111

THANK YOU FOR THE HUMILITY AND INSPIRATION

CHRIST OUR LORD, GOD OF HEAVEN AND EARTH.

Robert and Eugenia Hulett, Katherine Hulett, Nadia Hulett, Ross and Barb Feder, Anthony Uhuegbue, Walter and Ruth Dodge, Monsignor Patrick M. McDowell, Rev. Frank Melovasich, Rev. James Hayden, Sister Mary Christa Kroening, O.S.B., Sister Benita Hayden, O.S.B., Sister Mary Paul Ludwig, O.S.B., Sister Mary Hope, O.S.B., Sister Mary Jean Tuttle, O.S.B., Rev. Edward Sthokal, S.J., Rev. Patrick M. McCorkell, S.J., Rev. Robert Kroll, S.J., Rev. Larry Gillick, S.J., Rev. John M. Bauer, Rev. Michael O'Connell, Rev. Patrick Griffin, Rev. William Graham, Rev. Timothy Backous, O.S.B., and Rev. Arnold Weber, O.S.B.. Dr. Boyd Seevers, Dr. Jason DeRouchie, Dr. Michael Wise, Dr. Bradley Sickler, Dr. John Mayer, and Master of Arts in Theological Studies (MATS) Class of 2009: Michael J. Ambrust, Ashley N. Frerich, Stephanie E. Gates, Matthew W. Nettekoven, Laura L. Rand, and Scott C. Wildenberg.

CONTENTS

Introduction

The American people need to know that an important piece of the puzzle is missing within our nation's economic crisis. It has haunted the nation for decades and periodically recycles its way into the news as small bits and pieces of broken promises and deniable claims. Discrimination often lies beneath the surface of existing problems and eventually rises to media attention. The failed auto industry, Wall Street and the housing/foreclosure devastation, layered between high unemployment, declining job markets, and the ever-increasing employee layoffs, is no doubt taking its toll on the United States economy and consumer confidence. To overlook American history, funding three of the most expensive wars in the Middle-East and bailing out the nation's largest auto makers and financial institutions is a high price to pay. Many people do not realize that work-related discrimination also causes serious damage to the nation's economy. The fact that discrimination was not a priority for any candidate who ran in the 2008 presidential election is no surprise. Business, politics, and the struggling working-class middle-America are a mix of oil and water politicians are not able to blend. Most people are immune to the pain and suffering that discrimination inflicts on individuals and their families, much less the economic crisis it creates. The crippling effects of this epidemic are costing America billions of dollars. Honest Americans are being denied the right to earn livable wages, pay taxes, cover their medical expenses, and make invaluable contributions to a country in desperate need of revitalization. Discrimination adds more fuel to the fire in an economy already trillions deep in financial debt. *The deep recession that began in 2007 is here to stay for a long time.* An employers' market should not be defined as one that allows companies to profit at the expense of defenseless employees.

People of certain age, race, color, origin, religion, gender, and disability must not be subjected to employer interpretations of state and federal laws regarding Equal Employment Opportunity (EEO) Rights. The Equal Employment Opportunity Commission (EEOC) is required by the United States Congress to enforce fair labor laws and practices and protect the rights of all Americans, not just large corporations. *Injustice anywhere is a threat to justice everywhere.* (Martin Luther King Jr. "Letter from Birmingham Jail," April 16, 1963)

CHAPTER 1

WHO AM I?

AS I WRESTLE WITH THIS simple yet complex question, bitterness stirs inside, for I must once again defend my rights in the workplace. Does it really matter who someone is as long as he or she has legal residency, has experience, has qualifications, is physically able to perform the job, and is willing to work? For introductory and practical reasons, I am an American (United States citizen), a father of two, brother, uncle, son, nephew, cousin, neighbor, friend, referral, acquaintance, and recent graduate studies student. In September of 2007, I began a journey once again as a student seeking greater knowledge and wisdom in pursuit of a master's degree. Theology, specifically the area of apologetics, became my field of choice. Defending my faith and beliefs in the modern business world was not my first choice. However, I do believe it is my calling. I had hoped thirty years of experience as a business professional, manager, sales

1

representative, entrepreneur, inventor, and creative product developer/ marketer extraordinaire would have at least qualified me for some form of gainful employment. The list continues: I am a faithful, forgiving, loving, and compassionate Christian man willing to accept all people and their basic human rights. My intent is not to appear arrogant or overly eager to establish credibility; that is not the point; fairness and equality in the workplace is what equal opportunity is all about, regardless of one's age, race, color, origin, disability, gender, and religious background. Equality is not only a right; it is guaranteed by the law enacted by the United States Congress, which all employers, including government entities, public and private corporations, must adopt and enforce. All government agencies and private businesses must be held accountable to the same laws and regulations. No one should be above the law, including the government.

On August 11, 2011, I turned another year older in a jobless market. My thoughts are the following: how is it possible to survive another year of unemployment, underemployment, and discrimination without losing faith and my reason for existence? My two daughters wonder what is wrong me and why I am not able to at least secure some sort of temporary job. They are bothered by the fact that I have not been able to help them much financially over the past few years, and they cannot comprehend why I am still unemployed after four years. Calmly, I responded, *"As soon as employers are willing to interview me and offer some form of gainful (full-time) employment and benefits."* My daughters' questions and concerns are reasonable, and yet, employers continue to restrict or close doors on certain types of people as if we are carrying a deadly disease. *For me, watching the daily sufferings of my family is harder to bear than my own.* Thoughts of "Why me and not someone else?" rage through my mind. My family's questions and concerns are normal and what most reasonable people would expect. It is virtually impossible for anyone to empathize with individuals suffering from the injustices of discrimination if they are not affected by it, are sheltered from it, or are a part of the problem itself. An entire family can lose hope and fall apart when no one hears their cries of anguish. After a while, bitterness and resentment set in and form a wall between loved ones. Accusations and criticisms eventually divide the home, leaving victims unrecognizable to one another. Who are you, what are you, and what have you done to prevent our demise? Rejection is painful—it challenges our self-esteem and creates doubt within our self. How can justice be so nonexistent at times when we have such a rich nation full of diversity, freedom, hope, and opportunity? After all, that is the promise of the American Dream, is it not?

Spiritual giftedness is one of my redeeming qualities. Relying on God's care in difficult times is another. "The Lord secures justice for the oppressed, gives food to the hungry." (Psalm 146:7 New American Bible) It is like having faith the size of small seeds: when planted, they grow into magnificent trees, thus becoming the homes for nesting birds. Twice a year, I attend a men's spiritual (silent) retreat for three days. For those who do not feel drawn by the Holy Spirit or the power of an almighty God, it is only a weekend of quiet, relaxation, rest, and diversion from a world of chaos. On the first night of the retreat, seventy men of all ages (twenty to eighty years of age) are reminded that our presence here is not that of our own making, but a Calling by God to His faithful servants. For me, I find it impossible to overcome challenges and defeats without first realizing my weaknesses. Once entered into the retreat, I unload my baggage filled with broken pieces of my life. I ask God only for the grace and trust in His divine abilities to take these shattered fragments and create a mosaic. As my disposition becomes more focused on God's word, a spiritual energy provides hope and encouragement to go back out into the world as a better human being. There is a spiritual quote frequently referenced at every retreat by Teilhard de Chardin, and it is finally starting to make sense to me: "We are not human beings having a spiritual experience; we are spiritual beings having a human experience." It is like a taste of fine wine or earthly bread made from human hands and offered to all who are willing to accept it as inspiration. When I leave the retreat at the end of the three days, I never profess to be anything more than spiritual in my beliefs and nothing less than human in my daily existence.

Being forced to endure three failed investigations conducted by the Equal Employment Opportunity Commission (EEOC), and its silent partner, the Minnesota Human Rights Act (MHRA), based on age discrimination, is a crime in itself. In addition to the EEOC/MHRA failures was a failed discrimination case conducted under the state umbrella of the Minnesota Department of Labor and Industry (DOLI) and its divisional partner, the Minnesota Occupational Safety and Health Act (MNOSHA). This particular discrimination charge was not age related; however, it was based on retaliation for filing two safety complaints for which the employer was in violation. These violations of rights fell between the cracks of both federal and state government. During the legal processing of my first OSHA discrimination charge, my suspicions were confirmed. The close relationship the government had with the employer was discriminating in itself. In fact, it was so close that the average person could identify them as birds of a feather. The government provided too many legal loopholes for the employer to easily jump through. There were numerous regulations, statutes, laws, and immunities protecting large corporations from employee claims. It is no secret; laws are made and administered in such a way that they favor government and large corporations. Unless an individual has a lot of money, power, and connections, there is little justice. Federal and state agencies such as the EEOC, MHRA, DOLI, and OSHA are assigned by Congress to enforce laws and protect the rights and safety of the people, are they not? Yes and no. Not all people are protected by the laws. The government agencies do not have the support, resources, competence, and training to aggressively investigate and prosecute all employers in violations. As it stands today, the legal justice system is extremely biased and unfair. It does not protect the rights of all people as mandated by Congress. The real tragedy lies with our elected officials who are afraid—they are not willing to address unpopular issues, such as equal rights, fair employment, and safety. Speaking out against age discrimination or any form of discrimination is too risky. Why risk alienating large corporate clients and special interest groups that may harm re-election possibilities? I made numerous attempts to call attention to these Main Street issues. I knocked on the doors of congressmen, senators, and even the governor of Minnesota Republican Tim Pawlenty a former 2012 presidential hopeful. All were too busy to hear my concerns. However, I did receive a brief Dear John email response from Congressman Erik Paulsen of Minnesota's 3rd District. Here is what Congressman Paulsen had to say,

> Dear John: Thank you for contacting my office with your concerns. It is good to hear from you. In our fast-paced world, I appreciate the fact you took the time to share your views on issues of importance to you. You can be sure I will keep your views in mind should this issue be brought to the

House Floor for a vote. Americans have many ways of being able to voice their opinions to lawmakers. I am glad you took advantage of that right you have as a citizen. Thanks again for contacting me, as I appreciate hearing from you. Please let me know whenever I can be of assistance. Sincerely, Eric Paulsen Member of Congress.

This is what we call "Minnesota Nice." If you have nothing to say or do not want to get involved you react generically by sending a standard "boiler plate" response. Regardless, EEO laws, the people in charge of enforcing them (EEOC and MHRA), corporate ethics, policies, and procedures—age discrimination is a political Pandora's box. It is easy to understand why no Democratic or Republican candidate newly elected or running for election/re-election (Congress, Senate or in the Presidential race) for 2012 will address in-depth employment issues regarding age discrimination or any form of bias discrimination, underemployment, livable wages, denial of benefits, or unemployment, nor will they even consider amending any laws made back in 1958, 1963, 1964, 1967, 1973, 1990, or 1991. Why address something that stirs fear beyond comprehension, or better yet, motivation for involvement (lack of funding, support, and popularity)? It is much easier to turn a blind eye and plead ignorance than do what is right and just for all. When the economy tightens, discrimination dramatically increases. In fact, the EEOC reported job bias claims reached a record high in 2010 close to 100,000. A stagnant economy combined with massive layoffs and hiring freezes over the past four years are only some of the contributing factors.

Most politicians and perhaps a high percentage of prospering (younger) individuals today are immune to the issues and concerns of middle-aged workers. Many are probably tired of hearing about *America's aging baby boomers* every now and then in the news. However, in the end, discrimination does affect all people, including government officials, corporate entities, younger and middle-aged men and women alike, regardless of employment status. First of all, the American economy cannot afford to lose billions of dollars in taxable wages, purchased consumer goods, investments, and interests. Most important, there is fear that millions of older Americans will create a problem for the government when they begin to tap into social security benefits. Closer to home, it hits even harder and deeper. When someone you know and love is suffering from discrimination in the work environment, it affects an entire family, their friends, and their neighbors. No one wants to associate with unemployed individuals that have human rights problems. If people have not experienced discrimination personally, they cannot relate to the situation or help long term. Support groups, networking, referrals, employment agencies, online job services, and job fairs are fine, as long as they lead to some type of equitable employment. Unfortunately, today's job market in America does not value middle-aged (forty-plus) men and women and younger employees equally, regardless of the fact that in the not so distant future, American employers will experience a workforce shortage of qualified employees, if they have not already. According to William Novelli, Executive Director and CEO of *AARP Magazine*, the fastest-growing population in America is the "baby boomers", representing seventy-six million and growing. Novelli refers to the fifty-plus age group, which will double in size over the next thirty-five years. Over the past twelve years, I have witnessed and personally experienced employers who created disparities and fabrications as a means of justification for treating middle-aged employees differently. Supervisors/employers have a mindset that older employees correspond to low productivity, high resistance to change, old-school training, and extreme deficiencies in comprehension and motivation. A misguided perception exists; older employees suffer from what I refer to as the terrible too's—too slow (productivity), too costly (medical), too expensive (compensation), and too resistant (inflexible, not willing to change)—in today's contemporary work environment. Age has a stigma and a coined phrase: "You can't teach old dogs new tricks." I firmly believe that if you continue to take away an old dog's food and kick him once too often, he or she will eventually bite back.

No employer owes middle-aged men or women anything more than fairness and equality when offering employment opportunities, compensation packages, and benefits. It is fair to say that most, if not all, middle-aged job-seeking and working employees have accepted the grim reality of today's work environment. The job market is not the same, nor will it ever be as it once was twenty or thirty years ago. Most people agree with this and have accepted the market change. All that any middle-aged individual expects is equal treatment. Older employees must have the same opportunities in employment, compensation, benefits, full-time hours, scheduling, promotions, and time away as employers are providing to their other employees. If an individual is qualified, experienced (prior work history and education), physically able, and willing to accept the job position, hire him or her. It is as simple as that. After all, the United States government adopted equality and rights in the constitution and established the agencies (EEO and EEOC) assigned to enforce the laws to protect all people. It is a violation of rights, and it is inhumane for employers and supervisors to stereotype, assuming older workers are liabilities, unable to compete with younger employees. Employers deny benefits and opportunities because they feel middle-aged employees are not long-term assets. A little common sense along with a small hint of logic would prove that twenty does not equal forty, fifty, or sixty when life experiences, ethics, work history, skills, creativity, vision, education, patience, endurance, wisdom, and a void (shortage) in the workforce exists. I have two daughters of my own in their early twenties. They may think they know a few things about living, but they cannot possibly compress twenty or thirty years of life experience without first living them. It is impossible and a fruitless effort to think otherwise.

Discouraged and frustrated individuals have allowed employers to force them into accepting unfair labor practices in order to survive. If an attempt is made to question or challenge an employer's actions, employees find themselves caught between biased reviews and employment-at-will (EAW) termination process. Discrimination has not only denied decent people employment, it has also driven them out of communities, cities, and states. Some people think that moving to another suburb, city, or even out of state, away from the injustice, will eliminate the problem. That is far from the truth because discrimination is everywhere. Unfortunately, people and businesses are the same no matter where you live. According to Werhane and Radin (1996), "at will employees have no rights to due process or to appeal employment decisions, and the employer does not have an obligation to give reasons for demotions, transfers, or dismissals" (p. 451). The only thing that has the potential for change is a person's attitude and willingness to stand up for his or her rights. He or she can either stand up for justice or continue to fall for injustice.

A few years ago, while on a silent retreat, I noticed an inspirational poem framed on a wall in the gathering area titled *DESIDERATA*. I began to take notes on various verses when suddenly, out of nowhere, the director appeared, and he handed me an official copy. Most, if not all, of the poem written by author Max Ehrmann has a common thread that coincides with issues of age discrimination. The following verse speaks volumes to what I believe is at the core of the problem:

> Speak your truth quietly and clearly; and listen to others, even the dull and the ignorant; they too have their story. Beyond a wholesome discipline, be gentle with yourself. You are a child of the universe, no less than the trees and stars; you have a right to be here. And whether or not it is clear to you, no doubt the universe is unfolding as it should.

After thirty years, I discovered why this poem sounded familiar. *DESIDERATA* was reprinted and placed in the back of my high school (1972) yearbook. The only difference was that the author's name had been omitted.

CHAPTER 2

Equal Employment Opportunity (EEO)

EEO LOGOS AND INITIALS PROUDLY displayed on most, if not all, corporate (private and public) and government employment advertisements and job applications is standard policy. However, all government entities must not only endorse EEO laws as goodwill ambassadors, they must aggressively lead by example. In theory, corporate America should mirror the United States government, thoroughly embracing EEO laws and fully incorporating them into its daily culture. Possibly every potential job seeker views the EEO icons as a standard formality, giving little or no considerations to their significance and meaning unless he or she has been a victim of discrimination. With that being the case, tolerance, acceptance, and survival forces many employees (of different races, colors, ages, origins) to psychologically wave their rights in exchange for employment considerations. In my experience over the past twelve years, I have found many middle-aged people, myself included, in dire need of full-time employment and benefits. Covering basic needs of food, shelter, medical, and minimal living expenses was my main priority. It is safe to say that the average person is not assuming he or she will face unfair labor laws and practices by employers/management. Excited about the opportunity, most people are unaware of the fact that employers use various forms of discriminatory tactics beginning in the initial application screening/interviewing process.

I began to research and study human resource management and human relations over the last twelve years out of necessity. Within a short period, my suspicions were confirmed. There are human resource (HR) software programs designed and utilized to not only save time and resources—they have become a loophole for legal discrimination. Most medium to large employers have gone to some form of electronic application process that screens files, searching for specific information. The software not only qualifies prospects, but it also verifies and confirms information employers are seeking. Responses to education, graduation/year, years of experience in an area, number of years lived at current/previous address, in addition to ethnic/race questions (EEO data), for example, can supply sufficient information for an employer/HR to delete the file from current and future consideration. Who is going to check and verify if, in fact, middle-aged applicants are given the same equal considerations in the screening process as younger applicants? Employers seek legal advice about whom they can hire and fire to ensure things are done without violating the laws and rights of individuals. One extremely helpful tool for employers is the "employment at will agreement" that employees are required to sign. Once hired, an employer can terminate an employee without providing a reason. The common-law theory behind EAW allows employers the right to hire, fire, promote, and demote any employee (not covered under contract or statute) at any-time and for any reason they decide. The government agrees with employers and attorneys on these issues. However, if an individual can show proof of an EEO violation, by providing evidence in the form of documentation and witnesses, it *may* help in filing a timely charge in the future. Most people never file a charge, feeling they are at an extreme disadvantage (fear, retaliation, lack of resources and support), and they are right. The legal justice system in America does not accommodate defenseless, poor, and oppressed individuals, nor can it handle most equal rights violations and concerns for these people.

John Carlin, archivist of the United States, strongly supports EEO policies that create a work environment free of discrimination. He believes all employees should have the same opportunities to develop, perform, and advance to their fullest potential without having concern for race, origin, color, gender, age, religion, and disability. In an ideal world, this sounds comforting. However, a quick reality check will disprove this theory. An employer/supervisor can target an employee from a protected class under the EEO laws, using him or her for a short-term fix or as a cover-up to prevent and conceal a previous liability exposure without the employee ever knowing he or she was bait. Like company policies, the success of an EEO program weighs heavily on management's overall commitment and follow-through, with senior level management charged with enforcing and policing the plan. There is truth in the cliché *lead by example.* Unfortunately, this has become lip service for many employers/supervisors, while others appear to prescribe to the *do as I say not as I do* approach. It is extremely difficult to follow a leader/

supervisor whose actions are unethical, unfair, and in violation of state and federal law.

Abuse of authority is not only threatening and destructive to the individual employee and his or her family; it has a ripple effect that antagonizes other employees' morale and productivity. Case in point: a supervisor once commented to me, "You do not have to like someone in order to work with him or her." He was dead wrong. That comment alone cost my family and me substantial loss of compensation (salary, commissions, and bonuses), annual increases, benefits, and promotions. For four years, my supervisor provided little or no support while restricting business opportunities and leveraging various forms of disparate treatment that eventually cost my job. There was good news: he eventually resigned from the company. Unfortunately, for me, it was too late; the damage was done long before. My beliefs, values, and ethics did not align with the senior staff in charge, and the cultural environment of the company was such that it was impossible to rally support because the inaccurate information had already been communicated.

EEO laws encompass an umbrella of regulations and specific rules designed to protect people from discrimination. Title 29 C.F.R., Part 1614, contains regulations that govern the processing of federal discrimination complaints. In addition, there are definitions of the roles attorneys, managers, supervisors, and witnesses play.

While the legal terminology and lengthy formalities may be necessary, be aware: regulations and laws are written by attorneys for attorneys and judges (who are also attorneys) to interpret, agree with, or disagree with, as they have all the advantages of interpreting state and federal laws and Supreme Court decisions. It is difficult and impossible at times, for me to grasp or even accept the fact that law-abiding citizens have fewer rights and lower priorities compared to criminals. Why is this so? There is always the remote possibility a convicted felon was wrongfully charged and innocently incarcerated. Possibly his or her rights may have been violated and he or she cannot afford an attorney, in which case one is often appointed by the United States courts. The courts also allow criminals the right to an appeal via *pro se* legal representation (self-representation). Considerations may go as high as the United States Supreme Court. If a person's rights are violated and the person lacks resources (money and legal representation), the person has no voice in his or her defense; (non-criminals) do not have the same rights in our legal justice system.

President Obama has established a partial Civil Rights agenda of which is currently posted on the White House website: (http://www.whitwhouse.gov/agenda/civil_rights/.com). A bullet point under the heading Fight Workplace Discrimination is at least a small step in the right direction compared to the previous administration. Expanding the current laws will do no good if the agencies running them have limited resources for proper staffing, training, and enforcing federal and state laws.

Congress made the following acts to protect and defend the people from discrimination. The heart and soul of EEO laws are the following: Title VII of the Civil Rights Act of 1964 (as amended); the Civil Rights Act of 1991; the Age Discrimination in Employment Act (ADEA) of 1967 (as amended); the Americans with Disabilities Act, Title I and Title V of 1990 (ADA); the Rehabilitation Act of 1973; the Fair Labor Standards Act of 1958 (as amended); the Equal Pay Act (EPA) of 1963; and Title VI of the Civil Rights Act of 1964, Prohibition Against National Origin Discrimination Affecting Limited English Proficient Persons.

Each of these laws was written for a reason, and that was to protect and defend the rights of the innocent. The needs and reasons for these laws have not changed. Tragically, discrimination still exits and continues to plague our society. The differences in discrimination today, when compared to discrimination prior to 1964 (race, color, gender, and origin) are the added ingredients of age, disability, and religion.

Age and disability alone are affecting all people regardless of race, color, national origin, religion, and sex. What is most disturbing to me, and many middle-aged men and women fighting age discrimination in the work force today, is the imbalance of justice. ADEA and Title VII of the Civil Rights Act of 1964 are similar laws, yet judges continue to interpret the two laws differently. To ignore the facts—that America's work force is aging, disabilities are on the rise, and the country has become a melting pot of diversity—is not only a gross mistake; it is an economic disaster and an enormous liability to underwrite. Why do we continue to gamble with our children's and great-grandchildren's futures? It is no different than passing off trillions of dollars of debt, created by our generation's errors, ignorance, and neglect, to future generations. This is wrong; it is unfair and unjust. With the current laws in place, and the elected officials present to govern those laws, we should be able to amend, fund, enforce, and protect all people's rights. After all, these are the law[s] and the right[s] of the people, are they not?

In 2004, the federal government celebrated the fortieth anniversary of Title VII (1964–2004 EEO laws). I do not recall of any fanfare, celebration, or strong media coverage of an event as significant as this forty-year civil rights milestone. Not to add more rain on this monumental parade, fighting for equality in this country continues to be an uphill battle. I am compelled to list the following cases of race discrimination settlements that reflect only a small portion of the disease that continues to infest our country daily, with no cure in sight:

1. Target Corporation: **$775,000** Race/Retaliation Settlement, EEOC (1/26/07)

2. Tyson Foods: **$871,000** Race Harassment/ Retaliation Settlement, EEOC (11/7/06)

3. AK Steel Corporation: **$600,000** Race Harassment Settlement, EEOC (1/31/07)

4. Michigan Steel Tubing Co.: **$500,000** Race Bias Class Settlement, EEOC (6/8/07)

5. Walgreens: **$20 million** Race Bias/Discrimination Settlement, EEOC (7/13/07)

6. Ford Motor Company: **$8.55 million** Race Discrimination Settlement, EEOC (6/1/05)

7. Home Depot: **$5.5 million** Retaliation Harassment Settlement, EEOC (8/25/04)

8. FedEx: **$55 million** Racial Bias Claims/ Discrimination Settlement, EEOC (4/11/07)

9. Texaco: **$176 million** Racial Harassment/ Discrimination Settlement, EEOC (2/16/99)

10. Coca Cola: **$475.2 million** Racial Discrimination Settlement, EEOC (11/17/00)

11. Nike: **$7.6 million** Racial Discrimination Class Action Settlement, (7/31/07)

12. Wal-Mart**: $50 million+$54.25 million+$78 million+$172 million+$2billion** (pending fines) Settlements Gender Bias Discrimination Suits, Denied Employee Breaks, Lunch Breaks, Equal Pay (12/9/08)

13. Berg vs. Drug Enforcement Agency (DEA): **$20,00**0 Racial Profiling Settlement, Federal Government **[Denies Any Wrongdoing]**, ACLU Says First of Its Kind (8/9/07)

14. Gateway Funding Diversified Mortgage Services LP: **$2.9 million** fine for violations of the Equal Credit Opportunity Act. Charged higher fees and rates to blacks and Hispanic borrowers. Federal Trade Commission (FTC) agreed to suspend $2.7 million as a plea settlement and gave legal permission to **[Admit No Wrongdoing]** (12/29/08).

15. City of Minneapolis and its Police Department: **$740,000** settlement after rejecting $2 million settlement offer for racial DISCRIMINATION. Twenty year history of racial bias and discrimination and still went on record stating **[Settlement Does Not Admit Any Discrimination]** (4/11/09).

These fifteen cases are only the tip of the iceberg, a small drop in a deep well of injustice. Companies like Nike often settle out of court to avoid bad publicity and further expenses such as legal fees, settlements, and profit losses. Arrogance, greed, and selfish corporate image are the reasons Nike denied any wrongdoing or liability in this recent case. Correct me if I am wrong: is this not a conflict of interest? Violating the rights of the same people on whom Nike spends millions of dollars (in annual advertising) as a means to lure African-American buyers into their profit game is a crime. Discrimination is just another form of terrorism, here in America.

For me, the (Title VII) forty-year celebration was nonexistent, as much of my time and energy was consumed defending my own rights in an age discrimination case. Fighting disparities and various forms of discrimination in the workforce is no picnic, especially for a family of four struggling to exist. Being subjected to the daily sufferings of unemployment, underemployment (below poverty wages), basic living expense cuts, and life-threatening stress levels of a family in crisis is beyond reasonable. If I seem to lack enthusiasm about this occasion, it is because we have had forty-seven years to perfect civil rights (1964-2011)—with limited success. Yet, we still stand a great distance from the mountain of equality. Equal rights laws are made to apply to all people, not a select few. Title VII is not the only law needing support and help. ADEA and Americans With Disabilities Act (ADA) are similar discrimination laws requiring equal processing, investigative support, and government enforcement.

Bigots and racists are in every work environment, neighborhood, school, church, and social network across America. Just look around— our culture encourages discrimination by accepting disparaging comments and unfair labor practices at work. Fear of alienation and retaliation forces many to cave in instead of defending people's rights and upholding laws.

A co-worker once informed me that he would do anything to help me in a discrimination claim providing he did not have to admit to witnessing any violations and he refused to sign his name on any form or documentation. Is this what our society refers to as *winning through intimidation*? The point is that when laws and rights are being violated, it is a crime, and no one wants to get involved.

Within the last seven years, I have met with over five hundred people who have suffered greatly from discrimination. The adverse affects (financial, ethical, moral, inspirational, and spiritual) discrimination is having on people are silently killing their motivation to make a difference in the world. My conversations with them are typical, as all appear to experience the same injustices. Management and employees alike were allowed to make derogatory comments on race, color, age, gender, religion, and origin, for which they often had a well-rehearsed cover and justification for their actions. It was as though they believed the first amendment gave them the right and confidence to spin the truth.

A supervisor once chastised me for allowing people of color (blacks); middle-aged, overweight, and unattractive female applicants to have the equal opportunity (EEO) to apply for employment. To add further insult to injury, the same supervisor discarded the applications of recent applicants (blacks; middle-aged, overweight, and unattractive individuals) without concern to EEO laws or individual rights. Tragically, this sick and deranged supervisor not only had a criminal mind but also was able to cover his tracks by altering files and fabricating false and inaccurate information on select employees. His perfected devious behavior enabled him to skate around violations and liabilities while maintaining support from upper management, including human resources.

This situation is not unique, nor is the supervisor. Discrimination takes place every day with employers, both private and government, in every town and city across America. For the most part, it goes undetected, becoming hearsay—one's word against another's. A defense attorney would boldly argue this as mere speculation while the burden of proof rests heavily on the employee(s). Employers are innocent until proven guilty; even then, the laws allow companies to go on record *admitting no wrongdoing* after settling in or out of court for millions of dollars in discriminatory charges.

For the marginalized, justice is often delayed and rarely, if ever, served. The guilty parties buy their way out on technicalities, while innocent victims continue to bathe in the same pain (discrimination) day after day and year after year. The Equal Employment Opportunity Commission would like to continue to remain vigilant in eradicating discrimination, which most Americans would support. However, priorities are such that the failed U.S. Economy and Wars in the Middle-East have been the United States' main priority, and it consumes a majority of this country's resources. With the federal government providing limited resources, entities such as the EEOC must appear busy, selecting only a few cases for consideration (Title VII), while most receive little or no attention.

When the United States Congress enacted Title VII of the Civil Rights Act of 1964, the Americans with Disabilities Act (ADA), and the Age Discrimination in Employment Act (ADEA), they were not only addressing serious rights and concerns of the people at the time but also future generations. Congress was correct then and still is today in stating it is illegal to discriminate in any aspect of employment when it includes the following:

- Hiring and firing;

- Compensation, assignment, or classification of employees;

- Transfer, promotion, layoff, or recall;

- Job advertisements;

- Recruitment;

- Testing;

- Training and apprenticeship programs;

- Fringe benefits;

- Pay, retirement plans, and disability leave; or

- Other terms and conditions of employment.

In addition, there are various other discriminatory practices under the laws that include the following:

- Harassment on the basis of race, color, religion, sex, national origin, disability, or age;

- Retaliation against an individual for filing a charge of discrimination, participating in an investigation, or opposing discriminatory practices;

- Employment decisions based on stereotypes or assumptions about abilities, traits, or performance of individuals of certain sex, race, age, religion, or ethnic groups, or individuals with disabilities; and

- Denying employment opportunities to a person because of marriage to, or association with, an individual of a particular race, religion, national origin, or an individual with a disability. Title VII also prohibits discrimination because of participation in schools or places of worship associated with a particular racial, ethnic, or religious group.

While employers are required to "post notices" to all employees advising them of their rights under the EEO laws that the EEOC enforces and their right to be free from retaliation, do employers truly understand the meanings of these laws? In my experience, many employers have a limited understanding of the laws. Most supervisors do not even comprehend the amount of liability they expose their companies to on a daily basis. Defiance, ignorance, poor training, enforcement, and a lack of proper education from human resources is one of the major problem areas. Another problem area, and possibly the most important, is that not all management agree with EEO laws, and they then believe the laws do not apply to them specifically. It is hard to believe this is true, but it is.

The work environment with the greatest amount of discrimination is usually a regional or branch location miles from the corporate offices. All it takes is one poor manager, and he or she can violate more rights and destroy more careers of defenseless employees within a short period. Nobody from headquarter offices will ever know the complete story and truth.

A former manager commented, off the record, as he continued to violate the rights of employees, saying, "It is your word against mine, and I have the company's support."

There are company rules, policies, and procedures, and government laws to protect employee's rights, are there not? In theory, yes, but in reality, it is far from the truth. Try to answer these "how do" questions without a spin. How do employees defend themselves from a maverick type of manager who bends the rules to conform to his or her branch standards? How do employees reason with a political baron (a supervisor with the company for forty-plus years) who has been coasting into retirement for the past ten years? The most damaging: how do middle-aged employees rally support around younger managers who are in control and politically motivated to climb the ladder of success at the expense of others? These three scenarios are not only real, but they happen all too often with many employers.

Unfortunately, for some companies, the size of the organization, number of employees, and distance between branch offices and corporate headquarters play a key factor, allowing management to use illegal discrimination practices. A corrupt supervisor can fabricate, falsify, filter, delay, conceal, and cover up discrimination issues long before they become exposed liabilities.

In 2006, I worked for an unethical supervisor who not only made discriminatory and threatening comments, but he also performed illegal actions, fabricated false information on employee records, kept two separate personnel files, and falsified workers' compensation records. His philosophies were not only naïve; they were a violation of state and federal laws. He was a "do as I say, not as I do" kind of manager. If ever he was caught in policy conflicts or was remotely questioned for his actions, which was rare and only on extreme occasions, he would apologize and receive a token hand slap. His defense was always this: "Your word against mine." A majority of the time, he had all the support required from management (supervisors and HR), and he knew how to manipulate the system. Management recognized this manager as primary and the only point of contact and authority. All correspondence from corporate was either made, or relayed, directly to the supervisor—leaving vulnerable employees with little or no support.

CHAPTER 3

AGE DISCRIMINATION IN EMPLOYMENT ACT (ADEA)

WHEN CONGRESS MADE THE ADEA laws in 1967, I believe their minds and hearts were in the right place. However, it was impossible to assume the laws could, in fact, fairly and accurately maintain justice and order without providing adequate funding for staffing highly skilled intake and field investigators and making revisions as needed. As referenced earlier, the largest population in American history is the aging boomers. According W. Novelli (2002) of *AARP Magazine*, mature Americans represent 35 percent of America's population, hold 77 percent of the financial assets and 57 percent of discretionary income.

This is more than just a demographic revolution; it should be of great concern to all people in this country, especially representatives of the United States government. Many are aware, including those in the legal profession, that the Equal Employment Opportunity Commission is grossly understaffed and greatly underfunded. The agency is lacking resources to adequately staff, train, educate, and conduct successful investigations on all formal charges of discrimination. Lawyers representing employees agree that judges often raise the burden of proof standards higher for age discrimination cases than for charges claiming race, religion, gender, and other forms of discrimination covered under Title VII of the Civil Rights Act of 1964.

I have found this theory true in my experience. While defending my rights in an age discrimination case, both the District and Eighth Circuit Appeals Courts of Minnesota failed to look at all relevant facts under ADEA rules or thoroughly review all evidence required by law. Unsuccessful in attempts with both the District Court and Eighth Circuit Court of Appeals, I submitted my case to the United States Supreme Court (Washington, D.C.) in December of 2006 for review considerations. Surprisingly, by the first week in January 2007, I received a brief letter from the Supreme Court simply stating, "Request denied."

For me, disappointment was not only the fact that every door along the road to justice closed; it was the shock of finding out *fairness* and *justice* are next to impossible for the poor, weak, and oppressed. Most people cannot afford to defend their rights; therefore, the laws are structured in such a way that they are forced to wave their rights. There were no attorneys, EEO representatives, or EEOC and MHRA investigators supporting my claims. I had no money or media coverage to support my charge, and our legal system is such that it will not allow an individual (*pro se*) the same rights as it does highly paid attorneys.

Regardless of the fact that state and federal government offices provide do-it-yourself forms that allow individuals the right to represent themselves *pro se*, the courts will only allow individuals limited and restricted rights to proceed within a highly controlled legal system run by attorneys and judges.

The Age Discrimination in Employment Act of 1967 (ADEA) [sec. 621–634] protects individuals who are forty years of age or older from employment based on age. The ADEA's protections apply to both employees and job applicants. Under the ADEA, it is unlawful to discriminate against a person because of his or her age with respect to any term, condition, or privilege of employment, including hiring, firing, promotion, layoff, compensation, benefits, job assignments, or training.

It is also unlawful to retaliate against an individual for opposing employment practices that discriminate based on age or for filing a discrimination charge, testifying, or participating in any way in an investigation, proceeding, or litigation under the ADEA.

The ADEA law appears very clear, direct, and to the point. All government and judicial entities, attorneys, employers, and employees must interpret the same meaning as written. If only it were that simple, we could embrace the Golden Rule and eliminate the need for all civil rights laws. This is dreaming at best; the reality is that a corrupt and greed-filled society does not accept idealistic rules or laws without various interpretations. What is morally and ethically right does not make good business sense for many. Often, I find the need to reflect on a scripture verse that helps me prioritize living: "What profit would a man show if he were to gain the whole world and destroy himself in the process?" (Matthew 16:26, NAB)

All one has to do is look at today's news and see the messages our culture promotes. Many are profiting at the expense of others while at the same time depleting their own moral values and self-worth. Discrimination exists in the minds of those that believe they have the right to exercise abusive authority and control over the powerless, the poor, and the oppressed. The year 2007 marked a forty-year milestone for the Age Discrimination in Employment Act (ADEA 1967–2007). I wondered if the EEOC would remember to send me a birthday card along with an attached report that accurately details their progress in the fight for justice in the work place. They might have even included a small note of apology for failing in three out of three of my discrimination charges (2003–2006).

The EEOC's success ratio is not only disturbing; it is alarming to think most discrimination cases will never be heard, recorded, or investigated. It is much quicker to abandon charges due to low priority and a lack of funding than it is to pursue the rights of violated individuals. Thousands and possibly millions of middle-aged people like me are insignificant when standing alone. What news or motivation for justice exists when we fall below the priority radar? There is always a response for and against which state and federal staff attorneys can argue when defending laws, judges, government entities, and their actions. While the people may elect the government, those elected are not representing the same people when government errors and failures occur. For the most, the EEOC findings are exempt— immune from any form of civil inquiries, investigations, and/or legal recourse. The United States Supreme Court is the only judicial body that has the power, when it decides exercise its authority, to overrule laws and decisions made by the lower courts.

The Supreme Court can pierce the government's immunity veil if necessary.

There is some positive case news to share, although one should not view it as a major breakthrough. Our culture is nowhere near a cure. Once again, this is only a small drop in the bucket when looking at the deep well of America's growing epidemic:

1. 3M Corporation: Three Age-Discrimination Lawsuits with Settlements of **$3 million, $12 million, and one undisclosed agreement**, 3M **[Admits No Wrongdoing]**, EEOC (8-22-11)

2. Allied Signal Aerospace: **$7 million** Settlement, Age Discrimination, Company **["Admitting No Wrongdoing"]**, EEOC (11-11-99)

3. BNSF Railway Company: **$800,000** Settlement, Age Discrimination (4-3-07)

4. California Public Employees Retirement System[CalPERS]: **$250 million** Settlement, Age Discrimination, EEOC (1-30-03)

5. Honeywell International: **$2.15 million** Settlement, Age Discrimination (10-4-04)

6. Johnson & Higgins, Inc.: **$28 million** Settlement, Age Discrimination (7-29-99)

7. Minnesota Schools (2) Districts of Retired Teachers: **$682,000** Settlements, Age Discrimination; and other Minnesota Schools (5) Districts of Retired Teachers: **$450,000** Settlements, Age Discrimination, EEOC (11-7-05)

8. Stillwater, Minnesota, School District: **$1.12 million** Settlement, Age Bias, EEOC (8/21/06)

9. Thomson Consumer Electronics: **$7.1 million** Settlement, Age Discrimination, EEOC (8-17-99)

10. Foot Locker Specialty, Inc.: **$3.5 million** Settlement, Age Bias, EEOC (11/15/02)

11. General Dynamics Corp.: **$2.5 million** Settlement, Age Discrimination Class Action, EEOC (4/17/96)

12. Benassi & Benassi (Private Law Firm): Settled Age Discrimination Cases

   • Bureau of Census [U.S. Fed. Govt.]: **$400,000** Settled, Age Discrimination

   • Caterpillar, Inc.: ("Confidential") Settlement, Age Discrimination

   • Keystone Consolidated Industries, Inc.: **$1.5 million** Settlement, Age Bias

   • Nestle Beich, Inc.: ("Confidential") Settlement, Age Discrimination

   • Northwestern Steel & Wire Co.: **$1.5 million** Settlement, Age Discrimination

How can any state or federal government agency expect private employers to obey EEO laws if the governments themselves violate the rights of their own employees? Imagine being a schoolteacher (in Minnesota or the entire United States), dedicated, loyal, and underpaid for twenty to forty years, and the government discriminates against you when you finally qualify for retirement, as if our teachers here in America have not earned their rights in a challenging, yet undervalued field. Earlier, I indicated that the age discrimination cases listed, in addition to the race cases identified in the last chapter, are not an accurate representation of what is truly going on in our country today.

President Obama's campaign was all about change. He stressed in his acceptance speech and at the inauguration "change is coming America." Unfortunately for the millions of people still unemployed or underemployed change has not come as promised. I have sent numerous emails, faxes, and letters to President Obama in hopes that at least someone on his staff would acknowledge my struggles with basic human rights. Surely someone in Washington must have a sense there are countless people on mainstreet silenced by the chaos of the failed auto industry, financial institutions, massive layoffs, business closings, housing foreclosures, ponzi schemes, rising unemployment and poverty levels. Even though I find myself at odds by attempting to get President Obama's attention I have nothing more to lose. It is extremely important that employment discrimination become a higher priority along with the economy. My last letter to the President dated April 29, 2009 addressed the urgency;

Dear Mr. President:

You recently met with your cabinet to discuss ways of cutting waste and unnecessary spending in various government departments. A time line of 90 days was given for all to come up with a concrete plan for reduction and possibly elimination of costly government programs. My concerns along with millions of other Americans in this country is that there are government programs and agencies which lack adequate support including funding, staffing, competency, accountability, and commitment to enforce the laws and rights of the people. In this high unemployment and jobless economy many are forced to accept discrimination as a byproduct of the failed economic disaster. If you cut, under-fund, or assume the status quo of a certain government agency in need there will not be enough money to borrow in order to prevent another great depression or human rights catastrophe.

The Equal Employment Opportunity Commission [EEOC] is one of the many agencies grossly lacking evaluation, funding, staffing, and support to protect the rights of all people in this diverse melting pot of America. Job bias claims hit a record high in 2008 and that does not even begin to tell the real story of where discrimination stands in America today. Since 2002 my family and I were forced to suffer through three failed investigations by the EEOC and it was not due to lack of evidence, false accusations, or speculation on my part. As a 55 year-old professional I know when an employer violates the rights of its employees based on (age, race, color, origin, gender, disability, and religion). No man or woman should have to practice law, maintain high levels of wealth, or have connections within corporations or government entities in order to defend his or her rights in the work environment. If the people have no money or government support from the EEOC or any HUMAN RIGHTS agency there are no EQUAL EMPLOYMENT OPPORTUNITIES (EEO) or EQUAL RIGHTS.

No employer (small, medium, or large) public or private should have that much control and freedom in the job market to be able to terminate, deny benefits and promotions and job opportunities because of someone's age , race, color, origin, gender, or religion. Alexander (2008) reported that Wal-Mart violated over 2 million labor laws in Minnesota between "September 11, 1998, through November 14, 2008," had $2 billion pending in fines, and was ordered to pay $54.25 million in damages to 100,000 employees (StarTribune.com). It appears no politician or government official sees discrimination as an issue in this economy? Where was the government when all these labor laws—women's human rights were being violated? America will not get back on track economically unless all people are treated equally. All U.S. citizens must be given the same opportunity to support their families in order to build a stronger and peaceful nation. Please consider my plea to rid America of this epidemic. I welcome the opportunity to discuss in greater detail the basic issues that are affecting all Americans in one way or another.

Respectfully,

John K. Hulett
A Voice for All People
www.AgeDiscriminationAmerica.com

Our court systems continue to fill with numerous discrimination cases; many are pending new filings, scheduling, litigations, arbitrations, out-of-court settlements, summary judgments, and appeals.

Most cases will never make it to court for various reasons, and it is not due to a lack of merit. Some cases are obvious, as most individuals cannot afford an attorney or do not wish to subject themselves to any further injustices. Once a private attorney is hired, many people have financial difficulties filling the coffers of a greedy attorney/law firm who may or may not have been honest about their initial fees and case involvement. When the smoke settles, it is not about having an attorney or good case that demands justice; it is all about the money and politics. Winning is an added bonus for most, if not all, attorneys.

Several years ago, I had numerous disappointing legal experiences with various attorneys who played a game that involved questionable ethics and conflicts of interests. In one case, the attorney I retained to represent my interests negotiated a settlement without my knowledge. The settlement only covered his fees ($10,000) and no more. Within a day or two, my attorney informed me of the so-called deal/offer he received. I responded, saying, "Interesting how the so-called deal only covers *your* fees?" The offer was no deal for me.

Often, the difference between having a case and not having a case is money. As a means to test my theory, I asked my attorney how much money he would require to take my case to trial. He gave me a figure ($25,000) and informed me that if I could gather the funds, he felt good about the case. The truth is that it is not about winning or losing with an attorney. If a client has money, the attorney will always win, regardless of the outcome.

CHAPTER 4

AMERICANS WITH DISABILITIES ACT (ADA), TITLES I AND V

DO YOU EVER WONDER WHAT your life would be like if in the blink of an eye, you became disabled? Depending on the severity, the thought could be like losing your life or a parent, spouse, child, or friend without any advanced warning. Granted, no one can actually feel the daily pain and suffering millions of disabled Americans go through in this country. No individual or employer can feel the physical and emotional pain a person with a disability must endure.

The Americans with Disabilities Act (ADA) of 1990, Titles I and V (sec. 12101–12213) prohibits private employers, state and local governments, employment agencies, and labor unions from discriminating against qualified individuals with disabilities in job application procedures, hiring, firing, advancement, compensation, job training, and other terms, conditions, and privileges of employment. I would be remorse if I did not share some recent cases to see if, in fact, companies have taken the ADA laws seriously enough over the past nineteen years (1990–2009).

1. Sears, Roebuck, and Co.: **$6.2** Settlement, Disability Bias, EEOC (9/29/09)

2. Subway Franchise: **$166, 500** Settlement, Disability Bias, EEOC (7/27/07)

3. Starbucks: **$85,000** Settlement, Disability Discrimination, EEOC (2006/2007)

4. *Green v. State of California*: **$3 million** Settlement, Disability Discrimination (5/30/03)

5. Northwest Airlines, Inc.: **$510,000** Settlement, Disability Discrimination (12/30/04)

6. JPMorgan Chase & Co.: **$2.2 million** Settlement, Disability Discrimination, EEOC (11/22/06)

7. Wal-Mart: **$6.8 million** Settlement, Disability Discrimination, EEOC (12-17-01)

8. ConAgra Foods, Inc.: **$1 million** Settlement, Disability Discrimination, EEOC (5/20/03)

9. United States Postal Service: **$61 million** Settlement, Disability Discrimination (5/31/07)

10. *Ceimo v. Paul Revere, Provident Life and Accident, and General American Life*: **$84 million** Settlement, [**Denied Disability Benefits**] (4/2/03)

11. *Fisher v. Aetna*: **$8.6 million** Settlement, [**Denied Disability Benefits**] (7/9/98)

Just to add a little more icing to the cake, by fiscal year end 2005, the EEOC received 14,893 charges of ADA complaints. The EEOC resolved 15,357 disability discrimination charges for which they recovered **$44.8 million in settlements**. In addition, the agency boasts that since the beginning of ADA Title I and V (July 1992), EEOC has obtained more than **$600 million in settlements** for people under disability/discrimination charges. These figures do not include monetary settlements recovered through private litigations.

Quite clearly, it is obvious that employers have not progressed in the areas of ADA discrimination since Congress first enacted the laws (1990–2009). The United States Census Bureau, in a press release in December 2006, stated **51.2** million people were informed they had a disability, of which **32.5** million admitted to having *severe* disabilities. This should be of serious concern for everyone living in this country because people with disabilities affect us all in some way or another.

The amount of money employers spend annually defending discrimination charges, loss of creativity/productivity, legal fees, settlements, employee morale, and consumer awareness may not be enough resources to fund a five hundred billion dollar Iraqi War in the Middle East; however, allocating a small percentage (ten percent, or a five-billion-dollar reserve) could eliminate, or dramatically reduce, all discrimination in America. Possibly, it could ride on the coattails of an approved Homeland Security Budget with a special tag: *Domestic Terrorism/EEO Rights, Laws, & Enforcement.* Avoiding another disaster in this country will help create a stronger and richer nation. America cannot afford to incur more debt based on neglect and ignorance.

Imagine millions of middle-aged men and women in America with disabilities, mixed races, colors, genders, and various religious beliefs. Employers could potentially step into multiple legal landmines through either intentional or unintentional violations to individuals within the protected class under three separate laws: Title VII, ADEA, and ADA. If found guilty by a jury, employers could conceivably pay out millions and possibly billions of dollars in compensatory and punitive damages in addition to back pay, pain, and suffering. Should the media decide to seize the moment on any number of discrimination cases/multi-million-dollar settlements, this could ripple more bad news across the country, cutting deeper into the U.S. economy. Ultimately, this negative coverage could have an effect on consumer buying confidence and could lower trust levels even further regarding government entities and greedy corporations.

Saying that government and private employers are skating on thin ice with discrimination issues in this country is a gross understatement. While the ADA is very specific about the laws within its twenty-four pages of findings, in section 2 of 12101 there are two areas that strike a main nerve:

- (7) individuals with disabilities are a discrete and insular minority who have been faced with restrictions and limitations, subjected to a history of purposeful unequal treatment, and relegated to a position of political powerlessness in our society, based on characteristics that are beyond the control of such individuals and resulting from stereotypic assumptions not truly indicative of the individual ability of such individuals to participate in, and contribute to, society; ...

- (9) the continuing existence of unfair and unnecessary discrimination and prejudice denies people with disabilities the opportunity to compete on an equal basis and to pursue those opportunities for which our free society is justifiably famous, and costs the United States billions of dollars in unnecessary expenses resulting from dependency and non-productivity.

A good friend of mine, who has a disability, often shares his daily challenges along with his many frustrations and angers. He has type 1 diabetes, also known as juvenile diabetes, and it is serious, as his body does not produce insulin. With that being the case, daily monitoring of sugar levels and insulin injections is required. Stress, diet, exercise, rest, and the work environment all contribute to the physical conditions—with either high or low blood sugar as the result.

My friend meets the government's definition of an individual with a disability, and he qualifies for protection under the ADA laws. However, the employer games begin and end with their interpretation of what is making a "reasonable accommodation" to the known disability of a qualified applicant or employee if it does not impose an "undue hardship" on the operation of the employer's business.

My friend and I both worked for the same company and supervisor who cared little about government laws and company policies unless it applied directly to him or he could somehow benefit personally. Laws and policies were meant to be broken—or at least challenged. This was not only the philosophy of the supervisor; it was his operational protocol. To say that he had a criminal mind would be an understatement. I witnessed numerous violations of rights, laws, and policies under ADA, ADEA, EEO, and the company. I made many attempts to defend the rights of my disabled/middle-aged friend and failed. It was no surprise to me when the supervisor/employer denied any wrongdoing and, sadly, management and human resources stuck together like a band of guilty thieves.

What was most appalling was that the EEOC and MHRA agencies made no effort to conduct an investigation or thoroughly evaluate all evidence submitted, including the testimony of six key witnesses. From the outside, it appeared as though the government was protecting the innocent employer from guilty employees. After all, employees may have some rights, but employers and the government ultimately decide how much employees have and if, in fact, their rights were violated, or if they were just a fabricated myth. How it is possible that seven former employees lack enough credibility to stir some legal responsibility from the government is beyond me.

The United States Equal Employment Opportunity Commission is commissioned to enforce the employment provisions of ADA. However, the EEOC's guidelines are such: ADA rules *might* apply to job applicants and employees with diabetes. Therefore, in a sense, the door is wide open for employers and defense lawyers to argue favorably for themselves/their clients against charging employees. The following guidelines provide only a brief overview for employer considerations:

- when diabetes is a disability under the ADA;

- when an employer may ask an applicant or employee questions about his/her diabetes;

- what types of reasonable accommodations employees with diabetes may need; and

- how an employer should handle safety concerns about applicants and employees with diabetes.

The ADA/EEOC guide has good intentions, but in reality carries little or no weight with millions of Americans suffering from diabetes and other forms of disabilities, alienation, and discrimination in the workplace. There is a strong truth to the words *before you criticize and accuse, walk a mile in my shoes.*

According to the EEOC, seventeen million Americans from every race and ethnicity, from age twenty and older, have diabetes. I would venture to estimate a high percentage of the people with diabetes are in fact employed and functioning well, if not better than most without a disability.

No employer or supervisor has the right to predict or speculate future performance, attitude, and life expectancy of any human being. EEO laws are in place to protect employees covered under ADA, ADEA, and Title VII. Every American applicant/employee must be allowed the same rights and opportunities. There should be no argument to discredit the intent and factual reasoning behind the laws written by the United States Congress. In fact, most employees with diabetes perform their jobs extremely well and without employers ever knowing they have a disability. The accommodations required, such as regular work schedules, meal breaks, places for testing their blood sugar levels, or rest areas, cost employers little or nothing.

Back in May of 2009 I attended two Memorial Day Ceremonies held by our local Wayzata American Legion Post #118. The first ceremony took place in a neighborhood cemetery with honor guards displaying post flag colors, pledge of allegiance, laying of the wreath, prayer, keynote speaker, rifle salute, taps, and the raising of the American Flag. Two Young Navy Cadets in training handed out booklets sponsored by The American Legion simply titled *Let's Be Right on Flag Etiquette*. It was all about increasing public awareness on proper display and respect for the flag of the United States of America. It was well written providing numerous pictures and instructions for all ages to understand. The inside cover displayed four different yet effective photographs of the flag in settings such as schools, homes, government buildings, military situations. For some reason The Pledge of Allegiance defined in this simple way had greater meaning to me now than it did in the past:

The Pledge of Allegiance

This is our pledge to our country. You hear it a lot.
What does it mean?
"I pledge allegiance" – I promise to be true
"to the flag" – to the sign of our country
"of the United States of America" –each state that has joined to make our country
"and to the Republic" – a republic is a country where the people choose others to make laws for them. The government is for the people.
"for which it stands," – the flag means the country
"one Nation" – a single country
"under God," – the people believe in a supreme being
"indivisible," – the country cannot split into parts
"with liberty and justice" – with freedom and fairness

"for all." – for each person in the country…you and me.
The pledge says you are promising to be true to the U.S.A.
(THE AMERICAN LEGION and National Americanism
Commission)

If this is true for all Americans than the government and corporate America must hold themselves to the same truth. Liberty and justice means freedom and fairness for all U.S. citizens.

Laws are meaningless unless they are enforced. Innocent victims do not have the resources, support, and training of defense lawyers, federal investigators, federal judges, and Supreme Court Justices. How is it possible for disabled employees to defend their rights when the system itself is filled with bias and unfair procedures? Case in point: ADA laws and EEOC rules and regulations are posted on all government websites and are in most company policies, manuals, applications, and employee work areas. However, it is misleading as more and more employers/management teams find ways to undermine these laws, further subjecting employees to company/government interpretations. Employers have all the advantage and resources to mask violations and therefore deny any and all wrongdoing. It begins by setting unrealistic performance goals and reviews, and ends with forced suspensions, probations, and terminations.

I was informed of a situation wherein a disabled employee was called into to a meeting by human resources and management and informed of his alleged company violations. The employee was immediately suspended from work without pay for one week, forced into ninety-day probation, and was escorted from the building by security. This happened on a Monday morning prior to taking a lunch break. Once the employee realized he forgot his lunch, he went back to the office. Security notified management and human resources. Once again, the employee was reprimanded and warned not to return to the building until he had satisfied his suspension.

The company never made an attempt to accommodate this employee under the ADA laws. When informed of the disability, the company environment became hostile and discriminating in its actions. Prior to the alleged company violation, no other reported incidents or formal complaints, tardiness/late issues, or low performance standards had been reported. Early on in his employment, he made an attempt to share with management and human resources a formal notification regarding his disability, to which the company declined to listen and accept a doctor's recommendations. The supervisor chastised the employee for not informing the company about his [diabetes] disability during the interviewing process. That was *illegal questioning* and *violation of his rights under ADA laws.*

The ADA limits the medical information that an employer can seek from a job applicant. During the application stage, an employer may not ask questions about an applicant's medical condition or require an applicant to take a medical examination before it makes a conditional job offer. This means an employer cannot ask the following questions:

- questions about whether an applicant has diabetes, or
- questions about an applicant's use of insulin or other prescription drugs.

Only if an applicant voluntarily informs his employer that he has diabetes can the employer ask two questions: Does he need a reasonable accommodation? What type of accommodation?

This legally disabled employee was set up to fail. The company viewed him as a liability and chose to terminate his employment rather than provide accommodations. Was it wrong to assume the employer had an obligation to protect the health, safety, and equal rights of its employees? If so, what about our government? Who, in fact, represents the innocent employees?

CHAPTER 5

EQUAL EMPLOYMENT OPPORTUNITY COMMISSION (EEOC)

THE UNITED STATES EQUAL EMPLOYMENT Opportunity Commission has been given the authority and power to enforce federal laws prohibiting job discrimination. The specific laws within the jurisdiction of EEOC are the following:

- Title VII of the Civil Rights Act of 1964 (Title VII), which prohibits employment discrimination based on race, color, religion, gender, or national origin;

- The Equal Pay Act of 1963 (EPA), which protects men and women who perform substantially equal work in the same establishment from gender-based wage discrimination;

- The <u>Age Discrimination in Employment Act of 1967</u> (ADEA), which protects individuals who are forty years of age or older;

- <u>Titles I and V of the Americans with Disabilities Act of 1990</u> (ADA), which prohibit employment discrimination against qualified individuals with disabilities in the private sector, and in state and local governments;

- <u>Sections 501 and 505 of the Rehabilitation Act of 1973</u>, which prohibit discrimination against qualified individuals with disabilities who work in the federal government; and

- The <u>Civil Rights Act of 1991</u>, which, among other things, provides monetary damages in cases of intentional employment discrimination.

EEOC also provides oversight and coordination of all federal equal employment opportunity regulations, practices, and policies. Another note of significance: effective January 1, 1979, all functions relating to age discrimination administration and enforcement vested by section 6 (ADEA) in the Secretary of Labor or the Civil Service Commission were transferred to the EEOC under the President's Reorganization (Plan no. 1). Talk about having your plate full. This is not a good time for the most powerful voice of the American people to be understaffed, plagued with limited resources and restricted budgets. Sadly, it is an underestimation— poor planning and budgeting of our United States government.

It's no secret, job bias claims are at a record high. Discrimination claims filed with the EEOC in 2008 increased by 15 percent to

95,402 which at the time was considered the highest on record since the agency opened in 1965. The figures were up from 82,792 claims filed in 2007. By fiscal year end (September 30, 2010) claims rose to *an unprecedented level of 99,922.* In fact, caseloads for the EEOC increased by 15.9 percent between 2008 and 2009. According to Berrien (2011), "Discrimination continues to be a substantial problem for too many job seekers and workers, and we must continue to build our capacity to enforce the laws that ensure that workplaces are free of unlawful bias" (http:www.eeoc.gov/eeoc/newsroom/release/1-11-11. cfm). Retaliation claims have surpassed race as the most frequent filed by victims and the agency. EEOC claimed they secured over $404 million in "monetary benefits from employers" for fiscal year end 2010. The federal agency can justify the increase based on a bad economy. As more people lose their jobs it becomes a business casualty. This is another painful side effect of a deep recession.

The EEOC released figures showing age discrimination claims jumped last year by 28.7 percent to 24,582 while retaliation claims, those who felt they were fired or demoted due to other bias complaints in the workplace, experienced the second-highest increase.

Four years ago tragedy struck all too close to home and the horrific scenes of life and death continue to flash in and out of my mind. On August 1, 2007 (Wednesday 6:05 p.m.), a main artery through the heart of Minneapolis, Minnesota's freeway system, collapsed. The Interstate 35W bridge suddenly disappeared in the height of rush hour traffic. Generally, I watch the 5:30 p.m. and 6:00 p.m. nightly news. However, this day was different. I met with a friend late in the day around 4:30 pm, and went to dinner. It was 10:00 p.m. by the time I got home and my oldest daughter asked where I had been.

"Did you not hear the tragic news?" she asked.

"No," was my response, and I quickly turned on the TV for an update.

I could not believe what I was seeing or hearing from various surviving victims and rescue workers. My youngest daughter arrived home shortly after I was watching the tragic scenes unfold and informed me her friend was injured in a car accident when the bridge collapsed. Her friend suffered serious back injuries. The good news: she survived and would fully recover after much needed rest and therapy over the next four to six months.

My daughter informed me she was almost a victim of the I-35W bridge disaster. She and her friend worked together, performed in the same play, and normally rode together over the I-35W bridge. That day in particular, my daughter left work early and rode the city bus into Minneapolis in a different direction. She told her friend to go on without her that day, and my daughter would meet her at the theater by 6:30 p.m. By the time 7:05 p.m. rolled around, my daughter, the entire cast, and director's fears were confirmed. Every part in the play was vital, and so were the various roles played by each actor and actress. Even though the play was cancelled permanently, I was filled with gratitude for both my daughter and her friend. My mind may have been a little preoccupied with ADEA laws prior to the I-35 bridge disaster; however, it did remind me how fragile life and family are.

Early that day, long before the tragedy occurred, I prayed for my daughter's safety and asked God to watch over her that day. Miracles do happen when you least expect them. For me, miracles are a mystery, especially when they occur on the tail of a tragedy. My daughter and some of the cast gave a ring to their injured friend that says it all: "When you have faith, everything is possible."

There is a common thread between this fatal and tragic story of the I-35W bridge collapse and age discrimination in America. Historically and coincidently speaking, the I-35W bridge was completed in 1967 (forty-four years ago)—the same year the ADEA laws were enacted. Neither the engineers that designed the bridge originally, nor Congress, who approved the ADEA laws, could have predicted the amount of use, wear, and tear each would have to endure. No human-made design of any structure or law can possibly sustain the shifting sands of time, weathering and aging processes, without making frequent evaluations along with timely revisions and improvements.

It is extremely important that the EEOC has sufficient resources and the necessary tools for effectively staffing, training, contracting, and litigating (if necessary) all legitimate discrimination charges. If, in fact, the president of the United States and the Congress expect the EEOC to handle all its duties and areas of responsibilities thoroughly and in a timely manner, they must provide the tools—staffing and financial resources—to successfully run this program. Case in point: two key sections under the ADEA laws clearly spell out the authority of the EEOC:

- **ADMINSTRATION**
SEC. 625 (Section 6)
The Secretary (EEOC) shall have the power

> (a) to make delegations, to appoint such agents and employees, and to pay for technical assistance on a fee for service basis, as he or she deems necessary to assist him or her in the performance of his or her functions under this chapter;

(b) to cooperate with regional, state, local, and other agencies, and to cooperate with and furnish technical assistance to employers, labor organizations, and employment agencies to aid in effectuating the purposes of this chapter.

- **RECORDKEEPING, INVESTIGATION, AND ENFORCEMENT**
SEC. 626 (Section 7)

  1. The Equal Employment Opportunity Commission shall have the power to make investigations and require the keeping of records necessary or appropriate for the administration of this chapter in accordance with the powers and procedures provided in sections 209 and 211 of this title (sections 9 and 11 of the Fair Labor Standards Act of 1938, as amended).

Denying the rights and support of charging parties may be related to the fact that the government has placed unnecessary budget cuts, staff limitations, and priority restrictions on the EEOC. In theory, the EEOC has extraordinary power to yield justice, yet its authority to respond quickly and fairly to all complaints is extremely limited— narrow in scope for protecting all people from discrimination. In my eyes, it is a waste of government resources, an abuse of power and authority to allow one agency this much control, while shackling its abilities to legally, justly, ethically, and morally defend the laws and rights of all innocent people.

In the first chapter, I referenced three discrimination charges filed with the EEOC, all of which they failed in their investigations. Had the EEOC provided me the same considerations and fairness in its investigative findings as it extended to my former employers, this book would not need to have been written. Unfortunately, that is not the case. Budget restraints and staff limitations make it impossible to review with any detail, let alone investigate, most discrimination cases, especially age discrimination.

ADEA complaints have a tendency to fall between the cracks, giving them low priority and abandonment status. Problems surface quickly as investigators face the burden of case overload, time restraints, and internal pressures to resolve charges for statistical year-end records. I believe the EEOC prematurely labels the case when the initial charge is filed. The seriousness of the charges and level of priority assigned by the EEOC has already been decided. They leave a small opening for marginal legal and human errors. If the EEOC feels the initial facts of a charge support a violation of law, they may assign a priority investigation.

This is the rule: limited resources restrict the number of priority cases the government will consider. Another serious flaw in the system happens when the same investigator is assigned to investigate a similar complaint by the same charging party. This is a conflict of interest. Once a federal investigator has failed to successfully process a discrimination charge, the individual who filed the complaint is labeled—case/charging party lacks credibility and legal (attorney) representation. This is not to mention the fact there may have been personality conflicts, of which the investigator leveraged in prioritizing and closing the case.

When a charge is filed with the EEOC, the EEOC also "dual files" the charge with the state, which in my case was the Minnesota Department of Human Rights (MDHR) or Fair Employment Practices Agencies (FEPA). But ordinarily, the EEOC handles the charge themselves. In my three charges filed with the EEOC thus far, MDHR has not been a factor of any kind. MDHR sits quietly on the sidelines waiting for the EEOC to make its move and then rides the coattails of the EEOC once it dismisses the charge.

A Dakota County judge (Minnesota) ruled recently that an age discrimination suit (*Bogie v. Synergy Sources*) could proceed forward to court with a trial by jury. Currently, the Minnesota Human Rights Act antidiscrimination statute does not allow for a *jury trial* as per Minn. Stat. 363.14(2). According to Cummins (2007), "there are laws that allow for only a judge's ruling—so called 'bench trials'—often on the grounds that they are faster, cheaper and more efficient for everyone involved, attorneys said" (Star Tribune). Lawyers, of course, will appeal the decision, as they feel it to be unfair to their clients (employers). This is an employer's/defense lawyer's worst nightmare. The thought of facing a jury consisting of workers discriminated against is pushing the defense out of its comfort zone. In federal discrimination cases, trial by jury is allowed:

RULE 38. JURY TRIAL OF RIGHT

(a) **Right Preserved**. The right of a trial by jury as declared by the Seventh Amendment to the Constitution or as given by a statute of the United States shall be preserved to the parties in violate.

(b) **Demand**. Any party may demand a trial by jury of any issue triable of right by a jury by (1) serving upon the other parties a demand thereof in writing at any time after the commencement of the action and not later than ten days after the service of the last pleading directed to such issue, and (2) filing the demand as required by Rule (5)d. Such demand may be endorsed upon a pleading of the party.

For whatever hidden reasoning may be behind state statutes, wavering from federal laws and rulings are beyond my, and most people's, comprehension. Judges, lawyers, and politicians make the laws that only they seem to understand. The good news is that constitutional rights still hold a place in our legal system. My hope is that the people will continue to challenge current laws and demand equal justice within a legal system that has traditionally favored government and large corporations.

CHAPTER 6

Minnesota Department of Employment and Economic Development (DEED)

I BELIEVE THE INTENT OF the Minnesota Department of Employment and Economic Development (DEED) is to establish a goal that could hopefully create high-quality new jobs in Minnesota through promoting business creation, expansion, and relocation. The reality is that the cost of doing business in Minnesota is considerably higher for most employers when compared to other states in corporate taxes, unemployment taxes, and workers' compensation. Land, buildings, and improvements are at a premium. Minnesota ranks high in skilled wages as labor unions continue to maintain a strong foothold in the state. While some well-known companies (Best Buy, Target, Medica, 3M, and Sun Country Airlines) continue to maintain corporate offices, manufacturing facilities, distribution centers, customer service departments, and/or retail stores and outlets in the area, many others have left or dramatically reduced their labor force, wages, and benefit packages as a means of meeting competitive globalization standards and increased profitability requirements.

Do not misunderstand: Minnesota is a good state to live, work, and raise a family in. The state has some of the finest schools, colleges, hospitals, businesses, and research and development facilities in the country, if not the world. I was born and raised here; Minnesota is home for my family and me. However, like all states, it has its human flaws in both government and corporate areas and there is room for improvement. One such area is the Unemployment Insurance of Minnesota (UIMN) qualification and determination process.

The UIMN system is designed to primarily protect employers— not employees. If, in fact, benefits for an unemployed individual are approved, the process is not automatic. DEED forces pending applicants, many of which are already in desperate need of basic living expenses, to wait four weeks for final approval in addition to another one-week waiting period before the first week of earned benefits is paid. From this point, it takes three more days for a simple electronic transfer of funds to reach an applicant's personal checking/ savings account or approved state debit card. Billions of dollars are electronically transferred daily in this country—why can't the state government accommodate people in need in a timelier manner? Technology exists, and so does greed—using someone else's money for as long as possible is considered business as usual in America.

In a sense, employers and employees pay employment taxes to the state, where it is escrowed, regulated, and controlled. Unofficial user surcharge fees and penalty fines (delays and holding of funds) are added to help cover state budgets and shortfalls. The state never provides a detailed accounting of the total dollars that sit in the unemployment escrow account annually, the amount of unemployment benefits paid, or the balance unused. What happens to the millions of dollars in unused benefits? Only politicians receiving high incomes ($80,000–$200,000 annually), excellent benefit packages, lengthy vacations, and expense accounts ($60–$100 daily lunch allowances) know. When I was waiting desperately for unemployment benefits back in the fall of 2009 I sent a memo to Minnesota Governor Tim Pawlenty in hopes that he would reach out and help me. DEED was moving slowly in releasing federal extension benefits and if anyone could push government agencies along Governor Pawlenty could or so I thought. However, my memo may have left the Governor feeling a little embarrassed and out of touch with the average Minnesotan:

> As one of 16 million unemployed in America it was a small token of relief to have Congress and the President sign off on the recent extension of unemployment benefits for all states. However, the real disappointment is finding out our State [DEED] Rules are conflicting with those of the Federal. Minnesota penalizes the unemployed with its non-retroactive rules. DEED will not administer federal funds to unpaid weeks prior to the date it decides to establish as a qualifier (November 15, 2009). The unemployed are hurting enough as it is and yet we are forced to suffer even more by Minnesota's strict rules? These are the worst economic times since the Great Depression

and still state government stands on its firm policies while people are being denied basic human needs due to prolonged unemployment and weeks without benefits. This is morally and ethically wrong. No one volunteered to be unemployed, underemployed, uninsured, job biased, and poor. As the disparity gap widens in Minnesota and around the country who is going to look out for the fallen families on Main Street? We have inaccurate unemployment figures, outdated poverty measures, and government agencies lacking accountability, competency, and resources to enforce laws designed to protect the people. Last year Minnesota had over 500,000 people living in poverty and the mix of race, color, origin, sex, age, religion, and disability was all over the board. People are dying to live some form of basic human decency while politics either delays or denies this basic opportunity. Where is the Task Force in Minnesota to help those in desperate need?

Respectfully,

John K. Hulett
Life Long Minnesota Resident, U.S. Citizen,
Main Street American

By year-end 2006, Governor Pawlenty boasted of a $2.2 billion state budget surplus. Brief references were made by politicians and local news media about a possible tax refund for the people of Minnesota, but nothing happened. After the governor and state house representatives met in January 2007, the more than two-billion-dollar surplus quietly disappeared. The taxpayers of Minnesota never heard specifically what happened to this so-called surplus. One can assume that it was probably divided equally within the areas of great need: Minnesota Department of Human Rights (MDHR), education (school programs, teacher salaries), and Minnesota Department of Transportation (MNDOT) for road, highway, and bridge improvements. But this is merely wishful thinking on my part. As long as the tax base is improving and the quality of life is benefiting people living in Minnesota, most Minnesotans are willing to pay their fair share of taxes. It is interesting to note when Governor Pawlenty left office in 2010 in coming Governor Mark Dayton inherited Pawlenty's $5.1 billion deficit. This was not great news for Minnesota.

DEED attempts to stress the importance of unemployment insurance (UI) as an important workforce and economic stabilizer. UI is a temporary safety net, which allows qualified individuals the ease of transition into a new job. Employers should be able to benefit from having a qualified labor pool to draw from. However, in reality, employers who offer a higher, more competitive pay and benefits do not necessarily seek unemployed applicants from the Minnesota job force pool. Stereotypically speaking, applicants from the unemployed labor pool are not considered quality candidates in the eyes of many employers. Some companies view unemployed people as lacking in skill, experience, training, education, and motivation. The unemployed are not working for a reason; they are a problematic group of misfits that create greater risk factors and higher liabilities. The department began a survey program in 2002; it was conducted with individuals whose unemployment benefits were denied and others the state approved and paid. Interesting enough, in 2004, the department adjusted the weighting of the claims denied and those approved of which they supposedly made adjustments accordingly.

In my experience throughout the last five years, and from meeting with many unemployed and underemployed people, the department has raised the bar substantially, making it almost impossible for individuals to qualify for unemployment benefits.

Regardless of what the state may assume about employers and employment opportunities, discrimination is raging out of control. Assuming an applicant has earned sufficient wages within a one-year base period, he or she must be either partially or totally unemployed through no fault of his or her own. The following are reasons for disqualification:

- **Quit without a good reason caused by the employer:** Leaving for personal reasons or circumstances, not because it was the employer's fault.

- **Discharged for employment misconduct:** For actions such as continued, unexcused absences and/or tardiness; breaking company rules; neglect of duties; insubordination; being impaired by drugs or alcohol on the job; fighting; harassment.

- **Refused a job or failed to apply for a suitable job without "good cause":** For refusing work that was suitable for you based on work history, training, skills, ability, the pay scale in the local labor market, the distance to the job, and how long you have been out of work.

- **On strike:** When off work because you are a member of a striking union or are participating in the strike by honoring the picket line.

DEED will hold employees to strict rules and guidelines, statutes, and laws in order to protect employers' unemployment rates, control escrow funds and data recorded for year-end statistics. One major way to keep Minnesota's unemployment rates low and the state attractive to new business locations and existing business expansions is to restrict the flow of unemployment benefits. Employers support the local economies with growth plans once they feel government has their best interests (cost control and profitability) at heart.

A few years ago, DEED denied my unemployment benefits for the same reason they favored the employer: "Quit without a good reason caused by the employer." An adjudicator (state employee/administrator of unemployment benefits) first denied my benefits formally, and I filed an appeal, which was assigned to an unemployment law judge (ULJ). A telephone hearing was scheduled. The state position is that by eliminating travel expenses and lengthy in-person trials, employers, employees, and taxpayers save money. In theory, it makes good economical sense—that is, assuming there are no biased decisions made, all evidence and witness testimonies are weighed equally, and there are no conflicts of interests favoring the employer(s) or state government. DEED hooked me on a so-called technicality, a citation, which covers MN Statute 268.095, subdivision 1, in part: "An applicant who quit employment shall be disqualified from all unemployment benefits ... except when: (1) the applicant quit the employment because of a good reason caused by the employer as defined in subdivision (3)."

Subdivision 3 provides in part:

(a) A good reason caused by the employer for quitting is a reason
  (1) that is directly related to the employment and for which the employer is responsible;

(2) that is adverse to the worker; and

(3) that would compel an average, reasonable worker to quit and become unemployed rather than remaining in the employment.

If the state (DEED) ULJ, who is an attorney, and the defense attorneys assigned to defend the ULJ in the case of an appeal, are on a mission to deny unemployment benefits, they will find legal loopholes in favor of the state and employers. The average, reasonable worker referenced in subdivision 3(a)(3) is most often defenseless and lacking the resources to defend his or her rights.

In my case, I borrowed five hundred dollars and hired an attorney, provided five witnesses, and presented numerous files of evidence to support my claim. What should have been an hour hearing turned into three and a half hours, forcing the ULJ to break his rhythm and reschedule everyone for a second hearing three weeks later. There was no doubt in my mind; the ULJ was acting in the capacity of not only a judge, but also as defense lawyer and jury in favor of the employer.

No matter how much sound evidence and factual witnesses were presented in my defense, the ULJ/DEED was never going to approve my unemployment benefits. The attorney I hired was no help at all. He offered no defense in support of all the discrimination evidence (documents, exhibits, and witnesses) provided. Basically, he sat idle on the sidelines, thinking about his next case. As so far as the state goes, legal formalities were followed in that I was allowed the right to appeal the decision made by DEED/ULJ. DEED and my employer sealed my fate long before the first hearing. The hearings were only a means for covering a paper trail. After the second and final teleconference/hearing, the ULJ responded within three weeks affirming DEED's earlier decision, thus disqualifying my benefits. I requested reconsideration (review of all existing and new documents) and a "new law judge," as I felt there was a conflict of interest at this phase in the case. Requests were denied by both the director (defense lawyer for DEED/ULJ) and the ULJ. A notice of government immunity was sent along with the ULJ decision. Minnesota Statute *SS*268.105, subdivision 1, 5a, provides the following:

> Subd. 5a. **No collateral estoppel**. No findings of fact or decision or order issued by an unemployment law judge may be held conclusive or binding or used as evidence in any separate or subsequent action in any other forum, be it contractual, administrative, or judicial, except proceedings provided under this chapter, regardless of whether the action involves the same or related parties or involves the same facts.

Apparently, DEED/ULJ was not prepared to deal with an above average, reasonable worker who was not willing to give up his rights under federal (ADEA) and state (MHRA) laws without a fight. The State Agencies (DEED and MHRA) were not prepared to deal with a detailed discrimination case—reserved for the EEOC. DEED only reviews quick and simple (black and white) determinations based on employee layoffs or quitting. To pay or not to pay was the question. By denying my unemployment benefits of $9,490, DEED was able to retain the funds within the pool of unused benefits, which could be earmarked for some other state budget shortfall.

An appeal was filed with the State of Minnesota Appeals Court within 30 days of my benefit denial. Considering I had no resources to hire another attorney I represented myself *pro se*. The appeals court did not allow me to participate in an oral hearing, which involved a panel of three state judges. A non-oral hearing was to have taken place July 5, 2007, and the panel of judges had ninety days from the scheduled date to respond with a formal decision. This is a senseless delay of justice and an abuse of judicial power.

While a family of four continues to suffer, the government and employers conduct business as usual. It hardly seems fair that I am guilty and charged for a crime (quitting employment based on discrimination) while attempting to defend my rights and support my family. Was it a crime that I refused to allow an employer to continually steal my income, deny benefits, and accept a demotion to an employee twenty years younger? Employers are considered the real victims, innocent in the eyes of government until proven guilty beyond a reasonable doubt. Employees, on the other hand, are guilty as charged having only a remote possibility of justice.

By coincidence, while at a local library, I met another middle-aged unemployed man. The power went out in the building and the librarian came into the computer lab to inform everyone of the delays and probabilities of when the power would be back. The man next to me spoke about how he had nothing better to do and could not afford to drive somewhere else to find access to another computer. He was looking for work and applying online with a number of prospective employers. Frustrated, he spoke about being approved and receiving unemployment benefits, which the employer appealed and the state (DEED) and an ULJ overturned and ruled in favor of the employer. DEED/ULJ said the individual was disqualified from receiving benefits regardless of the fact the job was out of his field of expertise, had a thirty to forty percent pay cut, and was costing two to three hours more in (out-of-pocket expense) drive time. This is a gross misuse of judicial power and an immediate investigation should take place reviewing all denied benefit claims. Perhaps it's time to clean house in DEED: impeaching some of the ULJs that abuse their power and authority may be necessary or reassignment to clerk and administrative assistant positions might be an option.

To be frank, cleaning house in a governmental department is necessary. It is a common procedure that takes place when a new president takes office in Washington and when a new CEO takes over a corporation. The transfusion of new blood is necessary as the old is invariably contaminated.

Speaking of CEO's, I will illustrate a small reality comparison in a "too much-too little" ironic situation. While scanning the local newspaper recently, I read the business section and focused in on the "CEO PAY WATCH: General Mills Inc." To shed a little light on an overcast day, I wanted to compare my income for year-end 2006 with the CEO of General Mills:

CEO Total Compensation: $23,035,921, versus
My Total Compensation: $18,351

CEO Salary: $1,241,250, versus
My Salary: $17,351

CEO Non-equity Incentive Pay: $2,513,531, versus
My Incentive Pay: $0

CEO Other Compensation: $520,398, versus
My denied unemployment benefits: $9,490

CEO Exercised Stock Options: $18,232,377, versus
My Stock Options: $0

CEO Value Realized on Vesting Shares: $528,365, versus
My Human Rights Values: $0

The exercise was not made to assume that I am more qualified or skilled to run General Mills and therefore should be compensated equally. My argument is not about whether the CEO is grossly overcompensated and/or has excessive stock options. The board of directors and shareholders approved the CEO's annual compensation and benefits package. It is all about entitlement, collecting what is earned and available—exercising stock options and rights. For me to compare myself with the CEO in his area of expertise is unrealistic and absurd. However, to deny someone's human rights and unemployment benefits is an unjust violation of laws for which violating employers and government entities must be held accountable.

CHAPTER 7

VIOLATING LAWS—
PROFITING AT
THE EXPENSE OF
VULNERABLE EMPLOYEES

WHILE REVIEWING A NUMBER OF articles on major corporate scandals in America, I found the prepared remarks of Attorney General John Ashcroft (2002) at the Corporate Fraud/Responsibility Conference on Enforcing the Law, Restoring Trust, Defending Freedom not only appropriate but timely for this chapter. In business, it is impossible to commit fraud, falsify records, alter information, and profit at the expense of employees without violating laws and the rights of many employees, shareholders, and clients. Much of what Attorney General Ashcroft references regarding corporate fraud in America parallels discrimination in the same cancerous form. The following statements should strike at the heart of every concerned American:

> A nation built of emigrants has bound together in respect for the rule of law, trusting that the law will be enforced fairly and consistently. In addition, the unity borne of this trust has made the United States the most powerful and most free—the most productive and most generous nation in the history of humanity.

> The malignancy of corporate corruption threatens more than the future of a few companies—it destroys workers' incomes, decimates families' savings, and casts a shadow on the health, integrity, and good name of American business. The success of the free market depends on a marketplace of integrity—a marketplace that operates on information of integrity. Reliable, truthful information is the unseen force that drives the economy.

> But when information is falsified, the invisible hand that guides our markets is replaced by a greased palm. The goal of law enforcement, then, is clear: information cannot be corrupted. Trust must not be abused. Confidence must be sustained. America's marketplace of integrity must never be contaminated by a culture of greed.

Discrimination is a form of greed that denies all people the same access to equal employment opportunities, including full-time wages, benefits, and career potential. Employers exploit and take advantage of certain employees who should be protected under the laws of Title VII, ADA, and ADEA. For example, Wal-Mart violated over 2 million labor laws in Minnesota over a seven-year period, had $2 billion pending in fines, was ordered to pay $54.25 million in a class-action lawsuit to 100,000 employees and no representative in state or federal government viewed this act of DISCRIMINATION offensive and unacceptable. Even Governor Pawlenty was silent. It took ten years to reach a small token of justice for all the injustices these employees of Wal-Mart were forced to endure. It took the federal government years to respond to the worst corporate frauds in American history. Devastating multi-billion dollar losses combined with thousands of innocent employees left without work, savings, and retirement has brought tremendous shame and distrust in this country. These are only a sampling of some the most tragic cases defining America's first wave of financial failure in business history:

- ENRON: **$65 billion,** Fraud/Settlement -5,600 Employees Lost Their Jobs (October 2001-2002)

- Arthur Andersen, LLP: Obstruction of Justice/Shredded Documents for ENRON - Corporation Forced Closure/ Dissolved (November 2001 – 2002)

- WorldCom: **$11 billion**, Fraud - 17,000 Employees Lost Their Jobs (March 2002)

- Adelphia Communications Corp: **$11 billion**, Fraud (April 2002)

- QWEST: **$33 million**, Fraud - Four Executives Caught (February 2002)

- Home Depot: **$1 million**, Kickbacks/Rebates/Four Merchandise Mgrs. (February 11, 2009)

- Tyco: **$150 million**, Stealing Compensation/CEO and Finance Director (June 17, 2005)

- Merrill Lynch & Co: **$200 million,** Fines/Fraudulent Research (April 28, 2003)

- Bear, Stearns & Co. Inc., Credit Suisse First Boston LLC, Lehman Bros. Inc., Goldman, Sachs & Co., J.P. Morgan Sec. Inc., Merrill Lynch, Pierce, Fenner & Smith, Morgan Stanely & Co. Inc., Citigroup Global Markets/Salomon Smith Barney Inc., UBS Warbug LLC: **$1.4 billion,** Deception/Fraud Penalities (April 28, 2003)

- Halliburton Corp.: **$7 billion**, Controversial Government Contracts/Overcharging (May 2002)

- Target Corp.: **$1 million**, Settlement, Demoted, Retaliated, & Fired National Guard Soldier/Employee (6/15/07)

In the face of such damage, prosecutors, investigators, and regulators do not have the luxury of time. We simply cannot afford to wait to challenge corporate corruption until jobs are lost, retirement funds are depleted and confidence is destroyed. (Attorney General John Ashcroft, September 27, 2002)

Truer words were never spoken in recent times. However, truth is relative, and the laws that hold us accountable to these truths do not equally apply to all people. When you read a news article about a CEO of a large corporation that has $11.5 million of special incentives/perks temporarily frozen, it is extremely difficult to show compassion when millions of people are being deceived, discriminated against, denied equal employment opportunities, unemployment benefits, health benefits and coverage; many cannot even afford to feed their families. Who really cares about the frozen assets of an executive when the rest of the world is struggling to survive? What in God's name is wrong with this country? It is extremely difficult to accept the fact that 50 percent of America's wealth is owned by the richest 1 percent.

Ben Stein was quoted at a business meeting as stating, "Our number one crisis is the 'looting of America' by greedy capitalists and politicians who lean more toward defense contractors and drug-company lobbyists than working stiffs" (*Star Tribune*, July 31, 2007). Were the American people not deceived a few years later by a second wave of corporate fraud and greed which ultimately sent this country into the worst economic recession since the great depression? Once again Washington failed to keep an eye on America and the people living on Main Street were left behind holding an empty bag. Here are some of the historical highlights defining America's second wave of financial disaster:

- Freddie Mac and Fannie May seized by the federal government takeover cost estimated **$200 billion** (9-8-08)

- American International Group (AIG) federal government took control with an **$85 billion bailout** (9-12-08)

- Washington Mutual Inc. (WaMu) seized by federal regulators—**largest failure in U.S. history** (9-26-08)

- World Savings Bank fourth largest bank in the country— **failed with mortgage losses of $36 billion**

- Lehman Brothers investment house—**Failed** (9-15-08)

- Bernard L. Madoff Investment Securities ("Bernie Madoff") **$65 billion Ponzi Scheme** (12-11-08)

- Tom Petters (Group/Companies) and associates **$3.5 billion Ponzi Scheme** (9-8-08)

- William McGuire (EX-CEO) United Health Group fraud case involving stock options backdating, **agreed to pay $895 million in class-action lawsuit settlement** (9-11-08)

- Denny Hecker Fraud and Conspiracy—**Defrauded lenders $80 million in loans plus $13 million in losses and still owes Chrysler Financial $250 million for defaulted loans.**

Equality and social justice are not about leaning too far to the left or right in politics. Enforcing the laws, ethics, and moral obligations of business leaders is a government responsibility and duty to protect honest working class people.

There are a number of large mass-retailers that increase their overall profits by reducing labor hours, employees, and benefits— while demanding more productivity from fewer people. Willingness to compromise safety and compliance rules in order to save pennies on monthly budgets is not a valid reason for justifying personal bonus increases. When a supervisor is asked why the company eliminated the use of forklifts in a high volume distribution center, saving money and "It is least costly to have a $90,000 worker's compensation claim" is not a valid answer. It is hard to believe that such a scenario is happening in the real world. It is wrong—a violation of safety laws and employment rights. Profiting at the expense of vulnerable employees is criminal.

The Occupational Safety and Health Administration (OSHA) does not care if a company eliminates the use of forklifts, nor do they have any guidelines to weight restrictions or weight lifting. Apparently, if weight is a concern, the only recourse is to call your congressman or congresswoman and ask him or her to raise your concerns at the next congressional session.

Unfortunately, tragedy and the loss of lives often are the only ways to get attention and support. When death and disaster strike, it is too late to reconcile with greed and safety delays. Even though multi-million dollar settlements are paid, there never will be a price that can replace the value of human life.

As the state and federal governments continue to sort through the I-35W bridge disaster in Minneapolis, Minnesota, there will emerge answers to the many questions. Hopefully the people responsible for this tragic event will be held accountable. If not by the government or the people, the media will press for some form of accountability. According to the *Star Tribune* (2007), "Minnesota's financial shortfall for road and bridge maintenance has been decades in the making, the result of complex political tensions, but the disaster may have changed the money picture at last."

CHAPTER 8

EMPLOYERS' DEFENSE TO AGE DISCRIMINATION CLAIMS

MOST AGE DISCRIMINATION CLAIMS ARE filed as *disparate treatment* claims, whereby the employee (plaintiff) argues he/she has received less favorable treatment than younger employees, due to his or her age. Courts as a rule have adopted the disparate treatment theory used in Title VII race discrimination claims when reviewing age discrimination cases. The theory was originally established in *McDonnell Douglas Corporation v. Green*, which requires the plaintiff in a case of age discrimination in hiring to show the following:

1. The employee belongs to the protected age class.

2. The employee applied and was qualified for a job for which the employer was seeking applicants.

3. Despite the employee's qualifications, he or she was rejected.

4. After the rejection, the position remained open and the employer continued to seek applicants with the plaintiff's qualifications.

Employers and defense lawyers are willing to agree on the first (protected age class) while the remaining areas are argued and supported in favor of companies through means of various legal loopholes. Education is a legal form of discrimination that many companies use to screen applicants, deny promotions, and to eliminate job seekers from employment considerations. Job postings often have specific educational requirements, which, for example, may include a bachelor of science degree in chemical engineering and a master's degree in biochemistry. This narrows the playing field and eliminates most candidates from considerations. However, this is not an unreasonable request from an employer if, in fact, the position requires the specific skill and knowledge. Most prospective job seekers understand employers have a right to seek applicants that have specific educational and background skills. However, problems arise when employers skate around qualified middle-aged employees and hire someone that is younger and less qualified. Lawyers will defend their clients' actions, stating that employers can hire whomever they please and take all the time necessary. They can reject all applicants regardless of age, race, color, gender, creed, origin, religion, and disability, providing it was done in a nondiscriminatory manner. In fact, ADEA has no problem with employers basing personnel decisions on "reasonable factors other than age." In addition, employers may take disciplinary actions for "good cause." For example, demoting or firing an employee for poor performance is reasonable and a way to get around age discrimination.

Demotions and terminations are areas where employers and defense lawyers generally have the most success. The EEOC and district and appeals courts typically favor companies that show records and files in support of their actions. The burden of proof does, in fact, rest heavily on employees. Employers, along with the government, know this. Even though the ADEA prohibits discrimination and does not constrain employers from exercising other means and forms of hiring, promoting, and discharging employees, employee wrongdoing is relevant when taking measures employers feel are well within legal parameters.

Under ADEA and Title VII, there is a burden-shifting procedure in order for a terminated employee to establish a *prima facie* (presumed to be true at first appearance) case of employment discrimination. The employee must first establish he or she (1) was a member of the protected age group, (2) was qualified for the position from which he or she was discharged, and (3) was discharged under circumstances that give rise to an inference of discrimination; the plaintiff [employee] has established a *prima facie* case of *unlawful age discrimination*. In reality, the American legal system rarely allows for an average (ordinary) man or women equality unless the person has money, notoriety, and above-average legal representation. Many criminals, celebrities, wealthy individuals, and legal professionals have mastered their way in and around the system.

Online at http://www.MSN.com, a posted story was titled, "Missing People Face Disparity in Media Coverage." It states if someone is kidnapped or missing, it helps to be the right race, age, social class, and gender. If not, the media will pursue other news more worthy of coverage (August 16, 2007). Unfortunately, our media discriminates the same way as employers and the government when it comes to looks, race, and age. Appearance does, in fact, make a difference in how much news coverage, attention the media decides to give a story, regardless of the tragedy and the individual involved.

Numerous attempts were made in my first case (age discrimination) to shift the so-called burden of proof over into the laps of a former employer and its defense lawyers. Though unsuccessful in defending my rights within our legal justice system, I still fought a good fight. Defending my rights by demanding fairness in the workplace was not just about me; it was for all the people afraid and unwilling to subject themselves to a legal system that favors large corporate/government entities. *The ultimate measure of a man is not where he stands in moments of comfort and convenience, but where he stands at times of challenge and controversy.* (Martin Luther King Jr., "Strength to Love," 1963) Trying to find balance between living a simple life and fighting to survive in a complex world can be fruitless. Yet, we must attempt to overcome what may appear to be impossible to achieve.

In her book, *Living Simple*: *Learning from Native Americans*, Wanda Lawrence writes, "Our people believe and practice equality. Sex or age does not bar council. Among our people, it is said: 'We are all the same height'" (1987). In our society, age, gender, and race still play a factor in how we treat each other. Inequality thrives in a world too busy to notice its ugliness. Without realizing, we embrace it as standard practice. Stereotypical suburban racists may feel problems follow people who belong to a protected class, who are just looking for a change of scenery. Wanting the same opportunity as everyone else is unreasonable for the average man and woman to expect.

CHAPTER 9

MINNESOTA DEPARTMENT OF LABOR AND INDUSTRY (DOLI)

IT IS MY BELIEF THAT the Minnesota Department of Labor and Industry (DOLI) and Occupational Safety and Hazard Act (OSHA) are government agencies that serve a need in most work environments. However, the time to sound the alarm for help and support from DOLI and OSHA is not after a fatality occurs in the workplace—it is before. Why does it take serious injuries or multiple deaths at a jobsite to get DOLI/OSHA and employers to agree a safety problem exits and immediate action must be taken to prevent future tragedies?

After experiencing two failed investigations with DOLI/MNOSHA, it appears to me that the agencies suffer from the same issues as the EEOC, MHRA, and DEED. Legal loopholes, government regulations, politics, and the fear of offending large employers/corporate partners are the main reasons. Other reasons stem from employee fears of retaliation, intimidation, job security, lack of support regarding the discrimination, and employee reluctance to get involved. When a crime is committed, witnesses are often nowhere to be found, or their stories conflict with what actually happened. For whatever reason, witness pictures become unclear and they seem to have short-term memories of various incidents. Fellow employees barely remember the victim's name and whether his or her rights were even violated by the employer.

While working part-time in a distribution center for a large well-known retailer, I was shocked and disappointed with management arrogance and ignorance towards employee rights and safety concerns. Since 2001, the job market has been what many term an *employers' market*. Companies have an overabundance of prospects seeking employment and limited positions available. Employers have become extremely selective and discriminatory in their selection process of potential candidates. An employers' market does not give companies the authority to violate employee rights and deny them a safe work environment. Regardless, employers have an obligation to provide a fair and safe work environment. Most corporate policies include EEO and OSHA laws in their employee handbooks, and all management is responsible for adhering to state and federal laws pertaining to equal rights and the safety of their employees. If that is not acceptable, the recourse is to file a formal complaint with the various government agencies stating how unreasonable the equality and safety laws are for business.

No employee can expect anything more or less than what the laws, rules, and company policies state. If the wages and benefits are stated clearly and fairly and the employer's handbook details policies and procedures that incorporate state/federal laws, the company is obligated to enforce the laws covering all its employees. For many, this may sound reasonable, yet a select group strives to elevate themselves above the law. Individuals like this cause unnecessary suffering, hardship, alienation, and fatality for many people who are just trying to earn a living.

All that I, or any reasonable employee, expect from an employer/ supervisor is respect, fairness, opportunity, safety, and to be treated as a human being—the basics. Is that too much to expect from an employer for an honest day's work? Apparently it often is. My supervisor at the time of my complaint was in over his head with duties and responsibilities for which he lacked experience, education, skill, and training. Possibly the most significant piece of the managerial puzzle was missing—people skills. Tragically, this continues to be an overlooked problem for many companies in the United States that are already burdened with tremendous liabilities. People skills are overrated and understated, with many assumptions that they can be taught in a formal classroom by a casual company rally meeting, or packaged in some form of do-it-yourself corporate software.

My experience over the past thirty-five years has convinced me an individual either has the gift of people skills or not. I say this sincerely, as not everyone has the ability to motivate, lead, attract, and retain good people. Most importantly, good managers know and understand common-sense safety laws, rules, policies, and the rights of all employees. It is unreasonable for a company to think they can fill a void in a department by placing just anyone in an authoritative position. Setting a manager up to fail is not only a faulty design; it exposes the company to tremendous liabilities. The actions of one individual can create a deep ripple affect, causing high employee turnover, moral and productivity losses, as well as increasing the company liability exposure from a few thousand to millions of dollars, thus tapping into net profits. CEOs and stockholders of every corporation fear hearing this sort of news, especially when the media takes note and features it as a headline story of the day.

A good supervisor must always be aware of company safety policies and procedures at all times. There is never an excuse for a company and its management team to violate and abuse the rights and safety concerns of innocent employees and consumers. Secondly, a leader must at least comprehend the basics of state and federal laws relating to equal rights and safety. This is mandatory. No company lawyer or supervisor should ever attempt to cover up legal responsibilities and obligations due to managerial ignorance and error. Fear, pride, and ego often take center stage after managers make their mistakes. Add a little peer embarrassment and guilt to the mix along with questionable ethics and legal ramifications. The game of denial and pointing fingers begins to unfold, and innocent victims fall from grace.

As referenced earlier, my work environment consisted of a retail distribution center with several loading docks for receiving fifty-three-foot semi trucks loaded with palletized and non-palletized merchandise. Depending on the season and time of year, multiple truckloads arrived two or three days out of each week. When each truck door was opened, the merchandise was most often packed so tightly it was literally falling out. Everything was unloaded by hand and redistributed on pallets, carts, and two-wheel dollies. There were no forklifts on site to lift palletized merchandise weighing anywhere from five to two thousand pounds.

My first common-sense question to fellow employees was this: Is there not at least one forklift for use? They laughed and smiled, explaining that management decided to eliminate the forklift to save the monthly expense. Management's bottom line justification was based on gambling with workers' compensation claims compared to monthly savings in rental/maintenance fees. When I expressed my safety concerns to two different supervisors, they politely brushed all concerns aside, informing me the company used logic and safety in making their decisions.

Aside from the forklift issue, other safety red flags began to crop up as we moved merchandise in, out, and around the warehouse. At the time, all the shelving was not anchored to the concrete floor, and merchandise was being loaded beyond the rated capacity. An unsafe customer service program was in effect, forcing employees to rush, ignoring safe lifting, locating, and retrieving of heavy merchandise. Employees were continually challenged and forced to work over and around cluttered aisles. The company provided no protective headwear and eyewear (hardhats and safety glasses) to shield employees from falling merchandise while loading, unloading, and redistributing various products. Fire extinguishers, sprinkler heads, and fire exits were blocked by overstocked merchandise, creating fire hazards on the first and second floors. Highly flammable plastic bags for recycling were being stored on a shutdown conveyor system, which, if ignited, could cause an explosion on both the first and second floors. The on/off switches to the main freight elevator were defective, meaning employees could be trapped inside. Last, but not least, the cardboard baling machine was being used to produce bales beyond the loading, unloading, and moving capacity of two adults.

For a moment, I thought, "Who the hell am I, and why should I be concerned about safety in a company that could care less?" Most, if not all, employees working in and around the unsafe work areas had become immune because of management's lack of concern. After all, it was just a retail job paying eight or nine dollars an hour with no benefits, no future, and no respect for the people that worked beneath the food chain of authority, prosperity, and opportunity. However, this selfish thought was not consistent with what I believed was right. Accountability and responsibility are a part of my value system. For example, if I, or a coworker, were injured on the job because of carelessness and reluctance to speak out about safety issues, do I not share some of the burden and guilt of my ignorance? It bothered me that no employees were willing to voice their safety concerns to management. The excuse, "What good is it? No one ever listens" was not acceptable to me, nor was sitting on the sidelines listening to idle gossip. Apparently, most employees would only react if their own personal safety were directly threatened. Typically, those are the people that have full-time employment (forty hours or more), full medical benefits, higher compensation packages, vacation and sick pay, and seniority. Part-time people, like me, had all the risks: no medical coverage, no full-time income to sustain a family of four, and no one's support when supervisors unfairly reduced or reallocated hours to other (younger) employees.

One evening while I was working with my supervisor and another coworker, we were lifting heavy pallets of merchandise by hand up to the second and third levels on the storage shelving. I informed my supervisor the materials were too heavy to lift without a forklift and the merchandise was beyond the weight capacity of the shelving. He basically ignored me and told me to keep working. The other part-time coworker was lifting with an injured shoulder that had happened at his full-time day job. Rumor had it he may have been hiding a prior worker's compensation claim. Was this not both illegal and a liability exposure to the company? Everything about this coworker, including his arrangement with the company, seemed mysterious to me and other employees. Still, no one questioned management about this safety/liability issue. Regardless, I kept lifting with the injured coworker and my supervisor until the coworker complained about his shoulder hurting and my poor lifting skills. I kept silent while we lifted the next pallet of goods. As we struggled to place the material on the top shelf, it dropped on my hand, almost crushing it. I yelled for both my supervisor and coworker to help lift the pallet off my hand. Luckily, my hand was only bruised and did not require medical attention. From out of nowhere, a safety supervisor came to my rescue, or so I thought, and asked what was going on. Before I could speak, my supervisor and the coworker vanished. I voiced my concerns about various safety issues, including the shoulder injury of the coworker. The safety supervisor assured me she would address both the coworker and my supervisor.

Less than thirty-five minutes later, my supervisor called me into his office for a private meeting. He expressed concern about what I had said to the safety supervisor. I told him exactly. He was extremely quiet, giving me no response. He got up from his desk and informed me to go back to the area where the incident occurred. Both he and the coworker appeared, and they told me to help them finish lifting the same items we struggled with earlier.

This defiance and/or ignorance bothered me. There was no excuse for this for this reckless behavior and willingness to risk the safety of any company employee, regardless of his or her employment status (part-time or full-time).

My supervisor began to aggressively push me to work even harder and faster for the remainder of the shift. The tactics he utilized were no surprise to me. He viewed me as trouble for the company, and he had begun the process of elimination. His actions were such that his plan would physically wear me down, psychologically intimidate me, and financially break me by reducing my hours. At that point, I could see the value of having a strong union behind me. A union could at least defend and support my rights while collecting their weekly dues. Since the company was nonunion, this was an unrealistic and ideological thought on my part.

That evening, I went home discouraged and shared what had happened at work with my family. Their responses were expected, in the sense that most people would have thought or responded the same way as I did when safety was an issue.

When I went to work the next day, it was business as usual. My supervisor started pushing me around the minute I clocked in, like nothing had ever happened. I shared the incident with other coworkers I thought were friends, but they had nothing to say. One coworker asked who was there to witness the incident/complaint. As I explained, he walked away smiling as though he knew something. By "something," I mean that what I experienced was only my imagination. It never actually happened—my word against management's. In other words, forget about it; the case is closed.

What was running through my mind was unacceptable. How could I look the other way and allow myself to become trapped in a situation that potentially could devastate an entire family? The thought of having unnecessary medical claims with no insurance coverage, no savings or resources to sustain a family of four was not worth the risk.

After work that evening, I went to a local library and began to research Minnesota labor (DOLI) and safety (OSHA) laws in addition to employee rights. The Web site http://www.osha.gov was informative. The Office of Investigative Assistance at the time seemed more than helpful with the information it provided on the whistleblower program. In addition, it offered various links to DOLI sites and whistleblower publications for both employees and companies to review. For the benefit of this particular chapter, it is important that my focus stay on the areas that pertain specifically to my case.

To remain focused on the areas that pertain specifically to my case, I have highlighted the following key areas of the program:

The Whistleblower Program

The Occupational Safety and Health Act is designed to regulate employment conditions relating to occupational safety and health and to achieve safer and more healthful workplaces throughout the nation. The act provides for a wide range of substantive and procedural rights for employees and representatives of employees. The act also recognizes that effective implementation and achievement of its goals depend in large measure upon the active and orderly participation of employees, individually and through representatives, at every level of safety and health activity.

To help ensure that employees are, in fact, free to participate in safety and health activities, Section 11(c) of the act prohibits any person from discharging or in any manner discriminating against an employee because the employee has exercised rights under the act.

A person filing a complaint of discrimination or retaliation will be required to show that he or she engaged in protected activity, the employer knew about that activity, the employer subjected him or her to an adverse employment action, and the protected activity contributed to the adverse action. Adverse employment action is generally defined as a material change in terms or conditions of the case; "discrimination" can include

- Firing or laying off
- Demoting
- Denying overtime or promotion
- Disciplining
- Denial of benefits
- Failure to hire or rehire
- Intimidation
- Reassignment affecting prospects for promotion
- Reducing pay or hours

Regulations

- 29 CFR Part 1977: Discrimination against Employees Exercising Rights under the Williams-Steiger Occupational Safety and Health Act of 1970

  Filing a Complaint: If you believe your employer has discriminated against you because you exercised your safety and health rights, contact your local OSHA office right away. Most discrimination complaints fall under the OSH Act, which gives you only thirty days to report discrimination. Some other laws have complaint-filing deadlines that differ from OSHA's, so be sure to check.

After filing my first OSHA complaint online, I received a call from a local representative within twenty-four hours. To me, that was extremely impressive and said a lot about how seriously this government agency takes safety and health complaints. The intake investigator sounded like a veteran who knew the laws, rules, and rights of employees extremely well. After confirming all the information within the complaint, he provided two options for consideration.

The first option consisted of filing a formal complaint, which he would forward on to another department for processing. The timeline ranged from thirty to ninety days, pending the urgency of complaint and caseload of the investigator. The second option was based on filing a non-formal complaint, which could be processed immediately. A letter would be sent via first class mail to the company local branch, outlining the alleged hazards and a specific time to respond to the complaint and investigation. The intake investigator referred to this second option as "Texas Hold 'Em"; it was a way to catch the employer sleeping on the job, so to speak. Fear of the federal government issuing fines may motivate a company's call to action. After asking a few more questions, I decided to go the Texas Hold 'Em route. My identity was supposed to remain anonymous and, if discovered, the OSH Act 11(c) was in place for my protection, or so I thought.

Within a week, I received a copy of the letter that was sent to my employer. Minnesota OSHA (MNOSHA) gave the company seven days to respond to the complaint. They also informed me they (MNOSHA) would not share the employer's response. However, MNOSHA did emphasize three important points in its letter:

1. If MNOSHA does not receive a response within seven days of the letter date of the appropriate action taken or

that no hazard exists and why, an onsite OSHA inspection will be scheduled on the matter. An inspection may also be scheduled if the information provided does not appear satisfactory.

2. We encourage employee participation in investigating and responding to any alleged hazard. We wish to remind you that Section 11(c) of the OSH Act provides protection for employees against discrimination because of their involvement in protected safety and health related activity.

3. According to Minnesota Rule 5210.0420 Subp. 2, you are required to post a copy of this letter and your response to it, for fifteen days, where it will be readily accessible for review by all your employees.

The company's defiance continued regardless of OSHA's laws, rules, and demands made in its letters/complaints. The company did, in fact, violate my rights under Section 11 (c) of the OSH Act and Minnesota Rule 5210.0420 Subp. 2. Three employees accused me of filing a complaint with OSHA. Various discriminatory tactics were leveled against me by management representatives.

Some of the following forms of discrimination occurred, including layoff, blacklisting, and denial of promotion, disciplining, denial of benefits, intimidation, reassignment, and reduction in hours. No present or former employees were willing to stand up for their rights to work within a safe and healthy environment. Only time will tell if my actions were worth the losses endured in wages, benefits, and alienation from family and friends.

What is the point of having safety laws, rules, and regulations if they are not fairly administered and aggressively enforced by the governing agencies assigned by the United States Congress? Why do large corporations continue to receive extreme favoritism and strong support from the government, whereas employees are deemed guilty of accusing innocent employers of false and inaccurate charges? Bureaucrats and defense lawyers will argue countless reasons and justifications of why they support the current justice system and how it conducts its investigations and findings. In other words, accept the fact that truth is relative and justice is ultimately God's jurisdiction—do not bother to challenge laws that are made and controlled by man.

My feelings about the legal justice system in this country are strong, and rightfully so. Based on the many injustices/violations that I have experienced and witnessed over the past twelve years in business and through employer negligent actions, it is time to speak out for true justice.

After MNOSHA completed its two failed investigations, one informal and the other formal, they sent a standard letter, basically washing their hands of the complaint. Their reason was that they could not prove employer discrimination and probable cause. However, the door was left open, allowing me the right to bring private civil action against the employer, which MNOSHA and OSHA would not be a party to. The EEOC and MHRA operate on the same principle, which in a sense lends credibility and support to the employer's innocence and defense.

To satisfy my curiosity and exercise my rights, I requested timely copies of the investigation files. Within forty-five days of my request, an envelope came in the mail along with an invoice from DOLI/MNOSHA for $113.80. The agencies had an obligation to inform me of all charges prior to sending any files. At least the EEOC provided that courtesy. In order for employees/individuals to appreciate what little rights they have, the fairness and the odds of receiving complete and accurate files is a crapshoot. The government (MNOSHA/OSHA) has the right to withhold most if not all relevant information that they deem protected under various laws and regulations. In the cover letter, MNOSHA approved (with an X) two areas of my request and denied thirteen files that fell under statutes prohibiting release.

Consider if, in fact, there is fairness, truth, and justice within the select files DOLI/MNOSHA released:

1. Interviews (not taped) were (supposedly) conducted individually with four managers while in the presence of the company senior attorney. After reading each manager's response, there is no question in my mind the information was biased, coached, and filtered prior to their interviews. It is rare, if ever, that companies and its management admit to any wrongdoing. These four supervisors were close friends and extremely supportive of each other. They denied any wrongdoing.

2. My interview (taped) was conducted by telephone, wherein the investigator wanted to make sure relevant information was properly noted and recorded for accuracy. To my surprise and disappointment, much of the information was inaccurate, false, misinterpreted, and misspelled. The investigator assured me that she was a veteran (nineteen years) and knew how to process and account for all the information gathered. According this investigator, taping my interview was for review and accuracy purposes, or so I thought.

3. Witness interviews (none): There were nine active employee witnesses listed in the complaints. No interviews or acknowledgements of their existence were referenced. Was this an error or oversight by DOLI/ MNOSHA? An

inside source informed me one key witness was interviewed by telephone while a manager stood by, listening to his conversation. No reference to this interview was entered into investigative reports and final analysis.

4. Between the company attorney and MNOSHA, there were twenty-one pages of faxed and email correspondence (filtered, blacked out, and deleted) that had little or no value to me once the legal cleansing occurred.

5. The company attorney in three letters to MNOSHA reinforced his defense line using legalistic jargon. False and inaccurate responses suggested to me that management figuratively dumped a truckload of cow manure in aisle number ten and a defense attorney was needed for cleanup/cover-up duty. Each letter contained the following statement: "The company reserves the right to change, add, or modify its response." In other words, they have an opened-ended defense that denies any wrongdoing, thus proving their innocence.

6. The company's attorney was not quite sure to whom he was (strenuously) denying all claims, as he kept referring to someone other than me. He referenced a different name, suggesting to me that he considered it immaterial in his scurrying to avoid a liability.

7. MNOSHA's final eight-page report was filled with various omitted, deleted, and blacked-out data that more than favored the company, leaving me in a no- win situation. The government was immune from any wrongdoing and so was the employer.

I began this chapter stating that OSHA's place is in the work environment. There does need to be an organization that looks out for the safety, health, and welfare of all employees. But, having said that, OSHA must hold employers accountable for the same safety standards, which include the laws, rules, and regulations OSHA is assigned to enforce. In addition, OSHA must be held accountable for its actions, which include making fair, accurate, and thorough investigations with all legitimate complaints.

Discrimination is a serious issue and concern for all employees. If the agencies are not there to police corporate entities, thus preventing abuse and violation of employee rights, then why exist at all? Employees value their safety, health, and rights in the workplace and they expect OSHA to, at the very least, show support in the event that employers violate safety laws and the rights of employees.

MNOSHA is a state agency working under the federal guidelines of OSHA. If MNOSHA fails to properly investigate claims filed against employers, charging parties have a right to petition federal OSHA directly. A letter must be sent to OSHA within ten days of the discharge notice received from MNOSHA requesting a review of investigative files. The official title is known as Complaint about State Program Administration (CASPA). In my case, I followed the procedures as required, and within ninety days, the federal government (OSHA) washed their hands in the same manner as MNOSHA. The second paragraph in their letter says it all:

Following our review of documents provided by MNOSHA, interviews of MNOSHA staff, and review of the State's Administrative Procedures Manual ADM 3.6B, dated July 2003, it has been determined that MNOSHA conducted a thorough and timely investigation of the discrimination complaint and made a final determination based on the resulting evidence.

One government agency (OSHA) is not motivated to find errors in another agency (MNOSHA). (That is an assumption—there are other ramifications.) OSHA's letter thanked me for bringing my concerns to its attention. Supposedly, my interests help them monitor the state program and maintain a program that is "as effective as" federal OSHA.

CHAPTER 10

LAW AND JUSTICE— SERVED EQUALLY AND WITHOUT PREJUDICE

WE HEAR ABOUT LAWS AND the legal system most often through the news media. This may only provide a glimpse of how justice is perceived. Family, friends, and neighbors can provide a more accurate view of how justice is served. In the case of a traffic violation, such as speeding ticket (fifty miles per hour in a forty-mile-per-hour zone), assuming it is a first-time offense, the officer may let the individual off with a warning or issue a ticket and fine. The alleged violator has a choice of either paying the ticket and fine (having the state post it on his or her driving record for insurance companies to view) or appearing in court to contest the ticket, pleading not guilty.

The judge or law clerk may show some leniency for a first-time offense and erase the ticket from the driver's record. Is this justice? And, if so, was it equally served and without prejudice? We might argue that it is only a ticket and everybody eventually ends up with one. If found guilty, admit the truth and pay the fine. For someone trying to work around the laws to avoid the guilty charge is a cop-out, no pun intended. Intentionally breaking laws is a violation; finding loopholes in the legal system in order to escape any wrongdoing is a crime and therefore punishable by law.

On August 2, 2007, the U.S. District Court in Springfield, Illinois, denied a motion by Wal-Mart Stores, Inc., to dismiss a lawsuit filed by a former Wal-Mart pharmacist, which arose out of his suspension for refusing to sell Plan B and other drugs he considered abortion related. Ruling in the decision in *Ethan Vandersand v. Wal-Mart Stores, Inc.,* Judge Jeanne E. Scott held that Vandersand has the right to proceed with his case against Wal-Mart under both the Illinois Care Right of Conscience Act and Title VII, the statute that prohibits employment discrimination. In what makes this case light up the sky, Wal-Mart's defense argued the Right of Conscience Act does not cover pharmacists (as pharmacists are not considered health care providers providing health care services) and Title VII does not apply, as it was acting on an executive order issued by the governor of Illinois. Thus far, it appears that the laws and some form of justice was served equally and without prejudice. On that day, David won a huge victory over Goliath, Wal-Mart, the world's largest and greediest retail giant.

My prayer was that this case move as swiftly as the legal system would allow and directly into the courtroom, where it could be tried before a jury of twelve. My hope was that the jurors would see the truth and facts and send a message loud and clear to Wal-Mart. Violating laws and the rights of the people must not be tolerated.

When recounting the various violations of rights that occurred with employer number two, it is difficult for me to accept how and why this company was allowed to go free without a single charge. Management continued reckless patterns of misconduct, which included violations of discrimination under current laws (ADA, ADEA, and Title VII), harassment, and threatening statements. The EEOC and MHRA (for reasons political and/or lack of resources?) refused to investigate my claims, sat idle with the complaint for more than a year and, finally, dismissed the charge. The problem was not a lack of strong evidence and factual witnesses. It was that the government agencies (EEOC and MHRA) assigned by Congress to enforce and protect the rights of seven employees, including myself, were not there to lend support of any kind. Like defense lawyers, the government can interpret laws and charges that defend and support their decisions. The EEOC can decide, without question, which level, if any, of priority actions it will or will not assume on any charge. They have legal protection over information gathered, as well as immunity from the consequences.

Laws can be made complex and confusing to interpret by the average person or as clear and simple in this country as government and lawyers decide to make them. Human rights laws should not be written to confuse, mislead, deceive, or deny equality and justice for all. It is unconstitutional. If an employer intentionally and knowingly violates the rights of its employees and charges are filed with the government, why is there silence? Where have the rights of the people gone, and now, who will become their voice? God only knows. Once again, I am reminded of a poem that is timely and yet powerful. The following parody fits this case:

GOD TOUCHED ME

A man whispered, "God, speak to me," and a meadowlark sang. But the man did not hear.

So the man yelled, "God, speak to me," and thunder rolled across the sky. But the man did not listen. The man looked around and said, "God, let me see You," and a star shined brightly. But the man did not notice. And he shouted, "God, show me a miracle," and a life was born. But the man did not notice. So, the man cried out in despair, "Touch me, God, and let me know You are here," whereupon God reached down and touched the man. But the man brushed the butterfly away and walked on.

Author Unknown

How often do we look for a sign, some kind of proof, or evidence that a claim is worthy of review and investigative actions? Perhaps my first age discrimination (charge number one) case was not packaged in a way the EEOC could identify properly. Having previously witnessed a failed investigative attempt by the EEOC back in 2003, I made sure sufficient dates, times, files, records, and witnesses were presented in a timely manner for the subsequent charges. In fact, the information supplied to the EEOC was overkill. The intent was to eliminate most, if not all, speculation and reasonable doubt, clearing the way for our government to find probable cause that the employer had violated federal employment laws. "Guilty as charged" should have been the case. Mixed feelings of betrayal, mistrust, and bias raged within me.

It was as if the company received a presidential pardon, an official courtesy pass for being a first-time discrimination-charged offender. This was extreme prejudice.

Favoring a corporation over violated employees was wrong and against the laws of the constitution. Why the EEOC failed to find the employer in violation of law and my rights remains a mystery. Denial of benefits, reduction in pay, demotion from a supervisory position, harassment, derogatory comments, age issues, disability discrimination, religious discrimination, retaliation, and threatening comments from a supervisor should qualify as discriminatory conduct by the employer. Still, the government refused to fully investigate the charges and evidence supplied. Under the current laws, the EEOC is granted immunity from private (civil) lawsuits and testimonies, and does not have to respond to its investigative findings. In my three cases, the agency was under no obligation to defend what it failed to process. Government attorneys defending the EEOC argued, "We [EEOC] are not a party to private litigations, and, therefore, have no interests in participation."

Are the enforcement agencies and laws established by Congress, EEO, EEOC, MHRA, DEED, Title VII, ADA, ADEA, EPA, and OSHA not designed to protect all people? If, in fact, they are, then why are the federal and state governments refusing to enforce the laws they are assigned to protect? Who is watching out for the people— the defenseless employees?

In order to add clarity to my complaints, some of the main points are highlighted below:

1. **EEOC Charge #001**: Employer was allowed to fabricate and alter data on its documents supplied to the government, which included federal judges (district and appeals courts) and its defense counsel. The agency

assigned a trainee with little or no investigative skills to handle the (failed) case. Both the EEOC and district courts refused to consider the numerous discrepancies within the data presented, and the United States Supreme Court refused to review or comment on the case.

2. **EEOC Charge #002**: The EEOC was presented with extensive files filled with evidence, in addition to seven witnesses, and never conducted any form of investigation. The agency held the evidence/files for over a year and dismissed the charge. The employer was never questioned or interviewed formally for violating the rights of at least fifteen employees.

3. **EEOC Charge #003**: This case had a conflict of interest, as it was assigned to the same investigator that failed to investigate the previous charge, **#002**. The employer never responded in a timely manner to the charge (within thirty days). At that point, the employer was running sixty days late in response. The EEOC sent a letter extending the employer's date another thirty days, which totaled ninety days altogether. Five months passed and no investigations were conducted, nor were any of the six witnesses contacted.

The United States Supreme Court reviews less than one percent of the cases filed and does not have to look at any case, regardless of prior rulings, lower court errors, constitutional considerations, or amendment concerns. District and appeals courts review previous case history, yet they have a tendency to weigh in favor of corporate defendants based on defense counsel findings. Once the EEOC decides to wash its hands of the charge, they send out a standard boilerplate legal document dismissing the charge and issuing a

"Notice of Right to Sue." If someone is fortunate enough to find an attorney willing to take the case pro bono or he/she can afford to hire an attorney, a suit must be filed within ninety days of receipt of the dated letter. Most people never file a suit, nor do they bother filing a charge with state and federal governments.

A story in the local newspaper gave some hope that, even though justice is blind at times, it is possible. According to Thomas Lee (September 5, 2007) of the *Star Tribune*, Allianz Life Insurance Co. of North America (Golden Valley, MN) appeared to be close in settling one of several class-action lawsuits. Allianz was accused of falsely promising people cash bonuses that never existed. The settlement may affect 60,000 senior citizens nationwide. A Hennepin County District Court judge will have to approve the final settlement. Let us hope and pray that the judge approves this settlement and sends a harsh message to Allianz, the violator, punishing them for their criminal actions. When corporate greed becomes so defiant and careless in its actions that it robs helpless retirees, the courts must show no mercy or leniency.

What is most interesting to me is that the same company, Allianz, terminated a friend of mine because he refused to fraudulently overbill Medicare patients. When he complained to management about his moral, ethical, and legal position, he was fired immediately and escorted out of the building by security. Like millions of honest working people in this country, my friend walked away helpless and discouraged. He was no match for the corporate giant and thus forced to accept this injustice. His argument: the company was too big to fight. it was their word (Allianz's) against his, and the company had all the power (management support, money, defense lawyers), and he had only himself.

JOHN K. HULETT

MIDDLE-AGED IN AMERICA:
WHEN CULTURE VIEWS AGING AS A LIABILITY

The largest population in America consists of middle-aged men and women identified as the aging "baby boomers" (born between 1942 and 1964). Every day, millions of middle-aged men and women go out into the workforce to seek new employment, reemployment, supplemental employment, unemployment benefits, underemployment, creative employment, skilled employment, temporary employment, legal employment, and equal employment opportunities as established by the Senate and House of Representatives of the United States of America. Congress established the Age Discrimination in Employment Act of 1967 (ADEA) and created a statement of findings with the purpose of ensuring the rights of older workers (29 U.S.C.A. 621-634).

There are serious problems with interpretations and enforcement of the laws, and the state and federal governmental agencies assigned to enforce, instruct, train, and deliver the message to corporate America are failing to do so. Many U.S. citizens working in Minnesota feel the system is failing to protect their equal rights in today's job market. The largest workforce in the history of America consists of middle-aged men and women who need full-time employment and medical health benefits to support their families and cover basic living expenses.

I speak from experience over the past sixteen years, during which my family and I have endured unemployment, underemployment, disparity, poverty, and inhumanity, in addition to numerous violations of rights under state and federal laws. My family has suffered the greatest from my discrimination in the workforce.

In a country as rich as the United States, no individual should be deprived of his or her rights and equal opportunities to work and earn a livable income. It is unacceptable when anyone in the prime of his or her career (earning potential) has to plead with employers for consideration for part-time or seasonal work in an attempt to cover a fraction of his or her basic living expenses.

Most major employers in America proudly display their equal employment opportunity (EEO) logos, mission statements, and policies as a means of covering liabilities and to meet state and federal minimum guidelines. Since 2002, the harsh realization that my middle age as a cursed liability in the job market has been a tough pill to swallow. This is true for many displaced job seekers I know from networking in the community. It is unlikely any middle-aged person can reinvent who and what he or she is physically and psychologically.

Experience and wisdom are two qualities that come with age. They cannot be purchased or degreed, gifted, or substituted for youth, greed, and ignorance. There is no age limit on government officials and representatives elected or running for office (including the president, vice president and Supreme Court judges). Yet a heavy burden is placed on middle-aged men and women in our society, forcing them to prove they are still worthy of the same job opportunities and rights as younger individuals.

The laws in the United States do not protect all people from age discrimination, particularly those who have no money or voice to speak out against injustice. Poverty, disability, oppression, sickness, and terminal illnesses are additional burdens many have to live with. I used my voice to plead for help from the United States Supreme Court in Washington, D.C., in the hope that the highest court in America would hear what the lower courts failed to consider. On January 8, 2007, the U.S. Supreme Court denied my request (petition for a writ of certiorari) for review of a case that was in conflict of similar cases heard in the lower (appeals and district) courts, which the Supreme Court overruled.

Age affects all people, men and women of every race, color, origin, and religious background. For some, money can provide a short-term delay of the aging process by way of cosmetic surgery, influence, and connections. This is not the case for most people. Laws established to protect the innocent, allowing them a safe and secure environment to equal employment opportunity and freedom, is what makes America a fair and rich country. It is my belief that most middle-aged Americans would like the same equal opportunities, the ability to continue making contributions, and some encouragement from employers for offering a wealth of experience and wisdom below market level—extreme bargain basement prices.

TODAY'S JOBLESS MARKET IN AMERICA

The global marketplace has forced employers of all sizes (public and private) to run lean and mean and work around the legal system. Human resource departments have been given more power and tighter specifications when it comes to job posting, hiring, and firing process. Often times, a department manager will consult with HR personnel regarding vacancies, additional recruitment needs, and budget considerations. The specifications that many employers prescribe consist of younger (female and male) employees between the ages of twenty-two and thirty-two, skilled in specific areas, educated (BA, BS, and MBA degrees), many of whom are often hired at or above the market price. Management sends hiring supervisors on fishing expeditions for luring and catching the ideal employees. They are instructed on how and what to look for in potential candidates.

Since 2001, many of my colleagues and I have received little or no response from literally hundreds of job applications placed. Thanks to the Internet, older candidates are experiencing legal discrimination via electronic pre-screen. With only the stroke of a key, applications and resumes are deleted—eliminated without a trace. Major employers hide behind EEO statements posted with their job listings. If employers find their job postings are attracting too many older candidates, they place the jobs on hold or temporarily fill with an employment agency and repost them at later date.

When older workers find themselves locked out of employment in the field of their expertise, survival forces them into entry-level positions and unskilled labor jobs, subjecting them to hostile work environments, discrimination, and poverty wages. America suffers a tremendous loss when an experienced workforce is denied equal access to job opportunities. The United States needs all of our human resources, young and old, for developing new technologies and innovations. Discrimination kills the desire and depletes the energy required to make creative contributions in this country, which many middle-aged employees have historically made throughout their careers. The real tragedy older workers face in today's job market is the perception employers have of people in the forty-plus age bracket as lacking motivation, enthusiasm, progressive thinking, and contemporary training. Employers often believe middle-aged employees cost more to insure, compensate, and terminate, so they avoid incurring the liability, regardless of experience and skill.

Probably the most destructive combination for the violation of the rights of middle-aged America is the remote branch locations run by managers who have little or no daily contact with their direct supervisors and human resource departments. They have the autonomy to deviate from corporate policies, which includes setting different hiring procedures, performance standards, training techniques, compensation packages, benefits, promotions, demotions, corrective action plans, and terminations. Whenever violations of rights occur, management denies all accusations. A fabrication of files and record falsifications appear as the employer builds its defense to discredit the employee's charge. Most cases of age discrimination that become newsworthy are large class-action suits (3M, Best Buy, and Wal-Mart) involving multi-million-dollar legal fees. Justice is less about doing what is right for people and the laws that were designed to protect the innocent; it is more about money and bending the rules to meet profits and policies.

THE SYSTEM HAS FAILED TO PROTECT THE RIGHTS OF ALL U.S. CITIZENS IN AMERICA

When someone believes an employer has violated his or her rights, he or she has the right to file a formal charge directly with the Equal Employment Opportunity Commission and the Minnesota Human Rights Authority (MHRA) is automatically included. The MHRA is a silent partner only riding on the coattails of the EEOC. If the EEOC makes an error in the investigative process, the agency is not liable for its actions, for which the charging party suffers. Once the EEOC washes its hands of a charge, it may give an individual the right to sue in civil court. However, in the real world, most people walk away disappointed with the system that has failed to protect their rights due to errors, lack of competency, an inadequate number of experienced investigators, or lack of resources to retain legal representation.

The U.S. Supreme Court is not interested in reviewing a case that may require reinvestigation of errors and possible clean up of a mess made in the lower courts. When faced with cases that involve errors, fabrications, discrepancies, and violations of rights, individuals acting *pro se* have no chance (let alone rights) for considerations in the legal justice system.

The Minnesota Department of Employment and Economic Development and the unemployment law judge failed to develop all facts in one of the cases for which they affirmed their decisions denying my rights to unemployment benefits. Age discrimination was a motivating factor in my demotion, retaliation, and hostile work environment, which was created by the employer. DEED favored the employer even though the employer's evidence and defense was conflicting, lacking, and weak in testimony.

The system (state and federal governmental agencies and the U.S. Supreme Court) has failed to protect the rights of innocent people while its own laws protect the system. Government laws should protect the innocent and punish those who violate people's rights. This is not the case for many middle-aged Americans, who are struggling to survive in unfair job/labor markets. The government must not turn its back on this problem because it will become a greater burden for all in the near future. As more and more middle-aged Americans find themselves unemployed and underemployed in today's discriminating job markets, employers are finding more ways to work around discrimination. It has been an employer's job market for at least the past seven years, and there is no question middle-aged job seekers are feeling the power and control of corporate America. Everyone suffers when discrimination thrives on the largest population in American history.

CHAPTER 11 ▓▓▓▓▓▓▓▓▓▓▓▓▓▓▓▓▓▓▓▓▓▓▓▓▓▓▓▓

AMERICA'S DIVERSITY
AND LEGAL LIABILITY

CORPORATE AMERICA LOOKS AT DIVERSITY as both a necessity and opportunity. Potential revenues in this diverse market were projected at $1.4 trillion in sales for 2007. Food for thought: I venture to say that no mass retailer would ever discriminate against people of a different race, color, religion, creed, age, gender, disability, or national origin if they have cash (U.S. dollars) or approved credit and are willing to buy from their stores. When tapping into this large multicultural market in the United States, greedy merchants are somewhat careful about biting the hands that feed them. However, if diversity happens to filter inside their organization, they passively attempt to embrace it on the surface only. My former employer wallpapered (figuratively speaking) diversity everywhere in the company. Branch locations, employee manuals, break rooms,

Web sites, and employee mailings were just some of the means the company used to show their commitment. Corporate lip service, a sort of *do as I say not as I do* approach, was what the company actually embraced.

There are hundreds, possibly even thousands, of definitions of diversity, and the legal profession will have its own (spin on) interpretations.

I have selected one definition of diversity that appears to represent the spirit of many, but not all agree with this statement:

Definition of Diversity

The concept of diversity encompasses acceptance and respect. It means understanding that each individual is unique, in addition to recognizing our individual differences. These can be along the dimensions of race, ethnicity, gender, sexual orientation, socio-economic status, age, physical abilities, religious beliefs, political beliefs, or, alternatively, other ideologies. It is the exploration of these differences in a safe, positive, and nurturing environment. It is about understanding each other and moving beyond simple tolerance to embracing and celebrating the rich dimensions of diversity contained within each individual. (http://gladstone. uoregon.edu, August 22, 2007)

On the surface, this sounds like a definition many groups and organizations would utilize. As a matter of fact, it appears to be a mirrored image of what most employers, government entities, colleges, and schools would incorporate into their policies and mission statements. I hope we are not too naïve in our thinking to assume the term *diversity* used in today's culture is a contemporary substitute for softening human rights issues. Diversity has evolved from the civil rights movement and the laws that Congress enacted under Title VII (1964), ADEA (1967), and ADA (1991).

Diversity must not be mistaken or misused as a cover-up to hide discriminatory violations and violators of those laws. Case in point: when I was working part-time in a retail distribution center, I approached my supervisor with a couple of questions and concerns about some recent diversity training I had completed. At the time, I was fifty-three years old, the oldest non-managerial employee in the department. Surprisingly enough, my supervisor responded, "Forget about diversity and training; it does not apply to you." This was the same company whose CEO boasted diversity as being embedded in company culture and expressed throughout its mission and values. How can a company value its diverse employees when its own management refuses to embrace the company's commitment to diversity?

There is no excuse for employer greed, ignorance, arrogance, denial, and defiance of employment laws. Employers know the laws exist, yet they often refuse to adopt them. If a company allows its management to bend and flex its policies and rules, that is a problem. However, if the same company allows its management to violate state and federal employment laws, that is a crime and the company is liable.

Currently, there are no fines or fees levied on employers for violating employment laws. In many of the cases that settle out of court or in court, if they happened to be one of the fortunate, the employers have often gotten away with admitting no wrongdoing. If paying out multi-million-dollar settlements in discrimination suits is not admitting to any wrongdoing, then denying that EEO laws exist or that the rights of all people are guaranteed is only a myth. For more than forty years in this country, employment laws should have been protecting the rights of all employees. From the billions of dollars in settlements being paid out annually, the selective/passive enforcement of dated employment laws is costing all Americans.

In totaling the settlements I have listed under the EEO and EEOC for TITLE VII, ADEA, and ADA law violations, my calculations thus far total over **$1.7 billion**. A reminder: this is only the tip of the iceberg. There are millions and possibly billions of dollars in private settlements that never reach the news and recorded data files of the government. Even though the corporate fraud settlements are in a category of their own, the ripple effect does, in fact, touch every American in some way. Employers feel the government is too busy second guessing who's managing various agencies and departments. Total loss estimates for corporate fraud listed are over **$486 billion**. When you add the two settlement categories together, it tallies a grand total of **$487.7 billion** in gross misconduct fines, settlements, and bailouts. The spoils of excessive greed such as this could eliminate world poverty, create employment opportunities, improve healthcare and educational programs, and dramatically reduce discrimination as we know it in this country. Keep in mind this does not take into account the billions of dollars already spent bailing out the auto industry's (GM and Chrysler), other investment firms, mortgage lenders, and the estimated trillions for continued support and financing of three/four wars in the middle-east.

Politicians will argue reasons why we have discrimination in this country and debate about why we cannot fund more resources or revise existing laws and programs. I am not a politician, nor do I have aspirations of ever becoming one. However, I do have recommendations on how discrimination could be dramatically reduced and possibly eradicated from the American workforce. Treat discrimination like domestic terrorism and attack it from the inside. The enemy is either managing or working within various departments, including corporate and branch offices, and regional and field locations. Federal agencies must have the resources, training, and field expertise to counterattack all violations.

Some effective solutions to overcoming forty-four years of human rights violations are the following:

1. Equip all agencies (EEO, EEOC, FEPA, and state HRA) with adequate resources to handle caseload demand, including joint investigative work, if necessary. Double the field investigators, provide continuous staff training, and hire seasoned veterans of all (race, color, age, religion, and gender) backgrounds. Consider adding contract employees and consultants (human resources and compliance experience) to assist in timely processing of high-volume caseloads and shared field investigations.

2. Establish fines for violators with amounts pending levels of severity:

   (a) Gender: $35,000–$70,000
   (b) Religion: $35,000–$70,000
   (c) Harassment: $35,000–$70,000
   (d) Retaliation: $35,000–$70,000
   (e) Race: $35,000–$70,000
   (f) Age: $40,000–$80,000
   (g) *Disability: $50,000–$100,000

*In cases of intentional discrimination of people with disabilities and/or additional charges/violations (gender, religion, harassment, retaliation, race, and age), fines will be doubled, ranging from $100,000–$500,000 per offence.

1. Establish a Human Rights Tax Fund (for a three- to five-year period) and charge employers 1 percent of the company's annual gross sales/service fees, and hold in an escrow account similar to unemployment taxes—the differences would be that employers would have incentives for refund credits of 5 to 95 percent annually, based on zero charges filed with federal and state agencies. Companies that meet or exceed adopting compliance laws, testing, training, and certifications would receive additional tax credits.

2. Employers charged with violating employment laws will be listed on a public Web site for 180 days. Second-time offenders will receive one to two years of probation with specific government in-house training and counseling.

If you think this sounds extreme, then think about what it would be like for you and your family to suffer daily from lack of basic necessities, alienation, and oppression because of age, race, color, gender, religion, and/or a disability. Some people feel the death penalty is too extreme and believe that all life has value, regardless of the perpetrator's crime. Yet, punishing violators for failing to obey forty-plus years of human rights laws seems harsh? For more than seven years, anger, bitterness, and resentment have filled the walls of my home. There are times we end up blaming each other for things we have little or no control over. In my eyes, these are only some of the injustices that explode from discriminatory actions and violations.

Some time ago, I pleaded with a supervisor to stop undermining my efforts. He was stealing my income from customers and business opportunities I developed. My supervisor often assigned or divided my commission earned between either himself and/or select younger employees. No matter how direct and plain my explanations were, his eyes had no soul, no compassion, and no regard for human rights or any laws for that matter. Case in point: in the height of a busy season, he denied my income earned, and I argued the fact that he was hurting an entire family of four. My explanations were very clear; I could not support my family based on his discriminatory actions. His guilt was such that he had me step outside the store, and he handed me personal check for four hundred dollars. I do not want to sound ungrateful, but his check was only a small token of the several thousand dollars I was owed. Even with backup evidence, his word against mine was all the EEOC, MDHR, and DEED required for supporting the company's actions.

CHAPTER 12

AGING AND RIGHTFULLY SO

MY MOTHER HAD A FAVORITE song that she enjoyed listening to and singing along with while doing her daily chores as a full-time domestic homemaker. The song "When I'm 64" had a catchy chorus line, *"Will you still need me, will you still feed me, when I'm sixty-four"* (John Lennon and Paul McCartney, 1966). At the time, my mother would have been fifty-four, and she may have been thinking about her future and turning sixty-four. Her thought was this: *who, if anyone, will take care of me later in life?*

Though my mother never had to face age discrimination in the workforce, she was dependent on my father for support (needing resources for raising twelve children) and yet, at the same time, my father was equally dependent on her. Growing up during the great depression they learned quickly how to budget and survive long-harsh winters in Northern Minnesota. My father, on the other hand, did face harassment and discrimination at work, but he was from an era when people did not make grievances an issue (say nothing and keep it to yourself). ADEA laws were in affect (1967) when my father was working, and when he retired in 1974 after working at the United States Postal Service for thirty-three years, he just let go of his past employment concerns. In other words, he let sleeping dogs lie. To my mother and father, personal rights were more about enjoying home-cooked meals, celebrations (birthdays, weddings, Christmas, and Easter), and welcoming family, friends, and relatives. My parents were humble people, always grateful for the simple pleasures God provided. They were proud of every achievement made by their children, grandchildren, and great-grandchildren, regardless of how small or large. Married for fifty-three years, they never complained about not having enough money to pay bills or food to feed and our family.

Aging is inevitable, and all human beings do age to some degree a little each day. Marketing and research companies are diligently trying to figure out how to tap into the billions of dollars in wealth some seventy-eight million aging baby boomers have to spend. Over the past several years, many aging boomers have either lost or have been forced to use retirement and savings because of corporate fraud, rising health care costs, business loss(es), illness, disability, underemployment, unemployment, and discrimination. While there may be a level of some security with the people born between 1946 and 1951, there is a fair amount of struggle going on in this country with many born between 1952 and 1964. Failed businesses, lossed investments, devalued housing and foreclosures, mismanaged finances, and high divorce rates contribute to some of the problems. However, other factors, such as unemployment, underemployment, inflation, no health care coverage, high out-of-pocket medical expenses, food and fuel costs, and employment discrimination (EEO) weigh heavily on the minds of many middle-aged Americans. While there is no specific study that tracks this problem, it is a real growing epidemic in this country.

While at the library recently, I came across a job posting for the county. Simply, it stated, "Open Competitive, Custodian, Full-time, Benefits, Compensation: $12.88–$17.01 per hour." The qualifications were less than a high school education or up to one month related experience or training or an equivalent combination of education and experience. When comparing the overall package with a previous employer, the county appeared, at least on paper, very attractive. My former employer paid $9.00 per hour, offered only part-time work, and provided no benefits. Qualifications ranged from two to five years experience, high school and some college-level education preferred. As a rule, jobs with the county, state, and federal government are few and far between, and selective on hiring. In the real world, full-time jobs paying $10.00 plus an hour, including benefits, are extremely limited and screened for ideal candidates. It is questionable whether the good paying jobs actually exist. Or are many employers on a fishing expedition to see if, in fact, the right employee is available?

Employers have no idea of the amount of highly qualified and experienced talent sitting idle on the sidelines. Tragically, companies are losing millions of dollars in lost business opportunities by denying jobs to middle-aged applicants. All this highly skilled, creatively talented, well-educated, and thoroughly experienced personnel is wasting away, and for what—greed and ignorance?

My father was a man of deep thought, sharing little of his true feelings. He had goals and dreams like everyone else, yet he stayed humble in his works. One of his many writings and annotations over the years has been a great inspiration to me and my brothers and sisters. My father's notes were a reflection of who he was and, I believe, a piece of the remnant of who I am.

A man who works with his hands is a *laborer*,
A man who works with his hands and head is a *craftsman*,
A man who works with his hands, and head, and heart is an *artist*.

Robert S. Hulett, 1989

I am not sure what entrepreneurial potential my father possessed. But I know that had he pursued a dream of owning a business, he would have treated his employees with fairness and respect. Was my father denied the opportunity to utilize all his God-given talents? In some ways, yes—whether it was fear of risk, intimidation, and/or discrimination that deterred his dreams, no one will ever know. Had someone not discouraged my father (supervisors, co-workers, family) through unfairness, lack of encouragement, and support, who knows what he might have achieved? The same argument can be made about all forms of discrimination and how it robs the potential and opportunity from individuals that could have made a difference in this country. Just because a person reaches a certain age in his or her life or has a disability or perhaps a different race and color does not mean he or she has any less human value, skill, ability, and creativity to make a contribution in a world that desperately needs the help of all people.

Perhaps my voice has become that of my father and mother and all men, women, and children who have been silenced over the years out of fear and intimidation; let me become your voice for equality and justice.

Do me justice, O Lord, because I am just,
and because of the innocence that is mine,
Let the malice of the wicked come to an end,
but sustain the just, O searcher of heart and soul,
O just God. (Psalms 7:9–10, NAB)

The time has come for change in America, not because someone running for public office says so, but because it is our constitutional right, and fair-labor laws have been denied too long in this country. Individuals subjected to discrimination not only find themselves at a disadvantage in the job market but also lacking in basic living conditions. For the millions of people who have suffered from this injustice in the past and continue to do so today, we must stand up and let our voices be heard. If your rights are being violated, and opportunities are being denied, let your government (the United States Congress and president) know immediately. President Obama and Vice President Biden say they are committed to Combat Employment Discrimination. The people representing main street America must hold them accountable to their words if change is going to take place in this country.

Here is a list of government contacts for filing charges and voicing concerns.

The White House; http://www.whitehouse.gov/contact/.com Comments: 202-456-1111; Switchboard: 202-456-1414; FAX: 202-456-2461. You can call or write to the President:
The White House
1600 Pennsylvania Avenue NW
Washington, DC 20500

EEOC: Equal Rights (Title VII, ADEA, ADA) http://www.eeoc.gov; Phone: 1-800-669-4000; TTY device for hearing impaired: 1-800-669-6820; Email: info@eeoc.gov; EEOC Headquarters: U.S. Equal Employment Opportunity Commission, 1801 L Street, N.W. Washington, D.C. 20507; Phone (202) 663-4900; TTY (202) 663-4494

U.S. House of Representatives, 110th Congress: http://www.house.gov/ Contact your member of Congress

Write your representative

U.S. Senate: Senators' home listing of members' home pages, email addresses, telephone numbers and addresses, http://www.senate.gov/general/contact_information/senators_cfm.cfm

State Governors: http://www.usa.gov/Contact/Governor.shtml

U.S. Department of Labor, OSHA: Whistleblower Protection, http://www.osha.gov

Human Rights: Supporting Human Rights and Democracy, http://www.state.gov/g/drl/hr

Discrimination is an extremely important issue for all U.S. citizens especially, the millions who are suffering from unfair labor practices, long-term unemployment, underemployment, and lack of equal rights in this down economy. Remember, these government agencies and representatives are gatekeepers of the laws and protectors of the people's rights. Therefore, there must not be any compromise, or failure to enforce the laws that Americans hold as the truth. The voice of the American people must be heard now. It is time for change—all forms of discrimination must be incorporated in President Obama's 2009 CIVIL RIGHTS AGENDA.

References

Introduction

King Jr., M.L. (1963, April 16). In his own words, Martin Luther King Jr. Letter from Birmingham jail. *MSN Encarta*. Retrieved January 21, 2008, from http://spotlight.encarta.msn.com/Features/encent_Lists_default_article_MLKQuotations.html

Chapter 1

Ehrman, M. (1952). Desiderata. Retrieved August 23, 2003, from http://hobbes.ncsa.uiuc.edu/desiderata.html

Equal Employment Opportunity Commission (EEOC). (2011, January 1). Retrieved August 1, 2011, from http://www.eeoc.gov/eeoc/newsroom/release/1-11-11.cfm

New American Bible. (1970). New York: Thomas Nelson.

Novelli, W.D. (2002, February 21). Baby boomers: How aging boomers will impact American business. *AARP*. Retrieved July 7, 2007, fromhttp://www.aarp.org/about_aarp/aarp_leadership/on_issues/baby_boomers/how_aging

Radin, T.J., Werhane, P.H. (2003). Employment-at-will, employee rights, and future decisions For employment. *Business Ethics Quarterly* (Vol. 13, Iss. 2). Retrieved August 3, 2011, from http://www.jstor.org/stable/3857655

Teilhard de Chardin, P. (1929, October 7). The phenomenon of man. Retrieved August 3, 2011, from http://isgodcatholic.wordpress.com/2011/07/

Chapter 2

Carlin, J.W. (1998, July 22). Equal employment opportunity (EEO) policy. Retrieved July 20, 2007, from http://www.archives.gov/eeo/policy/

Civil Rights. The agenda. Retrieved April 22, 2009, from http://www.whitehouse.gov/agenda/civil_rights/

Equal employment opportunity commission (EEOC). Employers and other entities covered by EEO laws. Retrieved July 21, 2007, from http://www.eeoc.gov/abouteeo/overview_coverage.html

Equal employment opportunity commission (EEOC). Discriminatory practices. Retrieved February 9, 2008, from http://www.eeoc.gov/abouteeo/overview_practices.html

Equal employment opportunity commission (EEOC). Federal equal employment opportunity (EEO) laws: Celebrating the laws. February 9, 2008, from http://www.eeoc.gov/abouteeo/overview_laws.html

The United States national archives and records administration. Equal employment opportunity (EEO) laws. Retrieved July 20, 2007, from http://www.archives.gov/eeo/laws/index.html

Chapter 3

Alexander, S. (2008, December 9). Wal-Mart to pay $54 million to settle suit over unpaid work. *Star Tribune*. Retrieved December 10, 2008, from http://www.startribune.com/templates/Print_This_Story?sid=35819094

Crosby, J. (2011, August 22). 3M will pay $3 million to settle age discrimination suit. *Star Tribune*. Retrieved August 22, 2011, from http://www.startribune.com/templates/fdcp?unique=1314033658218

Equal employment opportunity commission (EEOC). The Age discrimination in employment act of 1967 (ADEA). Retrieved February 9, 2008, from http://www.eeoc.gov/policy/adea.html

New American Bible. (1970). New York: Thomas Nelson.

Novelli, W.D. (2002, February 21). Baby boomers: How aging boomers will impact American Business. *AARP*. Retrieved July 7, 2007, from http://www.aarp.org/about_aarp/aarp_leadership/on_issues/baby_boomers/how_aging

Chapter 4

American diabetes association. Type 1 diabetes. Retrieved August 3, 2007, from http://www.diabetes.org/utils/

Equal employment opportunity commission (EEOC). The Americans with disabilities act of 1990, titles I and V. Retrieved from http://www.eeoc.gov/policy/ada.html

Equal employment opportunity commission (EEOC). Disability discrimination. Retrieved January 1, 2006, from http://www.eeoc.gov/types/ada.html

Equal employment opportunity commission (EEOC). Questions and answers about diabetes in the workplace and Americans with disabilities act (ADA). Retrieved August 3, 2007, from http://www.eeoc.gov/facts/diabetes.html

Equal employment opportunity commission (EEOC). (2009, September 9). Press release: Sears, Roebuck to pay $6.2 million for disability bias. Retrieved August 1, 2011, from http://www1.eeoc.gov//eeoc/newsroom/release/9-29-09.cfm

The American legion. (2008). The pledge of allegiance. Indianapolis: National American Commission.

U.S. Census Bureau. (2006, May 12). U.S. Census Bureaus news, Press Release: More than 50 million Americans report some level of disability. Retrieved December 12, 2006, from http://www.census.gov/Press-Release/www/releases/ archives/aging_population/006809.htm

Chapter 5

Berrien, J.A. (2010, September 30). EEOC reports job bias charges hit record high of nearly 100,000 in fiscal year 2010, U.S. Equal Opportunity Commission. Retrieved August 1, 2011, from http://www.eeoc.gov/eeoc/newsroom/release/1-11-11. cfm

Cummins, H.J. (2007, August 19). Judge or jury? *Star Tribune.* Retrieved August 5, 2011, from http://www.startribune.com/ business/1121836.html

Equal employment opportunity commission (EEOC). The Age discrimination in employment act 1967 (ADEA). Retrieved February 9, 2008, from http://www.eeoc.gov/policy/adea. html

Minnesota Office of the Revisor of Statutes. (2005). 268.105 Appeals. Evidentiary hearing by an unemployment law judge. Retrieved October 15, 2006, from http:// ros.lwg.mn/bin/getpub.php?pubtype=STAT_CHAP_ SEC&year=2005&section=268.105

Minnesota Rules of Court. (2004). Federal, (VI. Trials). Rule 38, Jury trial of right. (pp. 37-38). Minneapolis: Thomson West.

Smith, M.L. (2011, August 2). Loved ones honored at I-35W dedication. *StarTribune.* Retrieved August 2, 2011, from http://www. startribune.com/templates/fdcp?unique=1312300634443

Tahmincioglu, E. (2009, March 9). Job bias claims rise to record. *MSNBC.com.* Retrieved March 9, 2009, from http://www. msnbc.msn.com/id/29554931/

Chapter 6

Minnesota Department of Human Rights. (2011). Retrieved August 9, 2011, from http://www.humanrights.state.mn.us/index.html

Pawlenty, T. (2006, November 29). Governor Pawlenty announces $2.2 billion surplus. Ninnesota North Star: Minnesota reference library. Retrieved August 5, 2011, from http://www.leg.state.mn.us/docs/2010/other/101582/www.governor.state.mn.us/mediacenter/pressreleases/

Minnesota Office of the Revisor of Statutes. (2005). Minnesota statutes 2005, 268.105, appeals. Retrieved October 15, 2006. from http://www/ros.leg.mn/bin/getpub.php?pubtype=STAT_CHAP_SEC&year=2005&section+268.105&keyword

Minnesota Office of the Revisor of Statutes. (2006). Minnesota statutes 2006, 268.095, benefit exclusion. Retrieved August 1, 2011, from http://www.revisor.mn.gov/bin/getpub.php?type=S&num=268.095&year=2006

Chapter 7

Alexander, S. (2008, December 9). Wal-Mart to pay $54 million to settle suit over unpaid work. *Star Tribune*. Retrieved December 12, 2008, from http://www.startribune.com/templates/Print_This_Story?sid=35819094

Ashcroft, J. (2002, September 27). Prepared remarks of attorney general John Ashcroft corporate fraud/responsibility conference enforcing the law, restoring trust, defending freedom. Retrieved August 10, 2007, from http://www.usdoj.gov/archive/ag/speeches/2002/092702agremarkscorporatefraudconference.htm

Davis & Norris, LLP. (2011). Securities fraud. Retrieved August 9, 2011, from http://www.davisnorris.com/securities_fraud.shtml

Patsuris, P. (2002, August 26). Accounting: The Corporate Scandal Sheet. *Forbes*. Retrieved August 9, 2011, from http://www.forbes.com/2002/07/25/accountingtracker.html

Singer, M. (2009, February 11). Home Depot Rocked by Kickback Scandal. *CBS News*. Retrieved August 9, 2011, from http://www.cbsnews.com/stories/2007/07/31/cbsnews_investigates/main3120258.shtml

St. Anthony, N. (2007, July 31). From, "The looting of America isn't funny, Ben Stein says." *Star Tribune*. Retrieved August 5, 200, from http://www.goldparty.org/benstein.html

USA Today. (2005, June 17). Timeline of the Tyco International Scandal. *USA Today*. Retrieved August 9, 2011, from http://www.usatoday.com/money/industries/manufacturing/2005-06--17-tyco-timeline_x.htm

Chapter 8

King Jr., M.L. (1963). In his own words, Martin Luther King Jr. Strength to love. *MSN Encarta*. Retrieved January 1, 2008, from http://spotlight.encarta.msn.com/Features/encnet_Features_Lists+default_article_MLKQUOTATIONS.HTML?G

DePass, D., Phelps, D. (2011, February 12). Hecker saga ends with no mercy. *Star Tribune*. Retrieved August 25, 2011, from http://www.startribune.com/templates/fdcp?unique=1314308109289

Thomson/West. (2005). McDonnell Douglas Corp. v. Green, 411 U.S. 792.93 S.Ct. 1817. 36 L.Ed.2d 688 (1973). Westlaw.

Chapter 9

U.S. Department of Labor. (2011). Occupational safety & health administration (OSHA). Complaints about state program Complaints about state program administration (CASPA), 1954.20. Retrieved August 9, 2011, from http://www.

osha.gov/pls/oshaweb/owadisp.show_document?_
ptable=STANDARD&p_id=11205

U.S. Department of Labor. (2011). Occupational safety & health administration (OSHA), Home. Retrieved August 9, 2011, from http://www.osha.gov/

U.S. Department of Labor. (2011). Occupational safety & health administration (OSHA). Office of the whistleblower protection program (OWPP). Retrieved August 9, 2011, from http://www.whistleblowers.gov/index.html

Chapter 10

Lee, T. (2007, September 5). Annuities face-off for Swanson and Allianz. *Star Tribune*. Retrieved August 10, 2011, from http://www.startribune.com/templates/fdcp?unique=13130157665229

U.S. Equal Employment Opportunity Commission (EEOC). (1967). The age discrimination in employment act of 1967 (ADEA). Retrieved October 13, 2005, from http://www.eeoc.gov/policy/adea.html

Sekulow, J. (2007, August 2). Federal court ruling acknowledges conscience rights of Illinois pharmacists. *ACLJ*. Retrieved August 8, 2011, from http://aclj.org/abortion/federal-court-ruling-acknowledges-conscience-rights-of-illinois-pharmacists

Chapter 11

University of Oregon, Gladstone. (2007, August). Definition of diversity. Retrieved August 9, 2011, from http://gladstone.uoregon.edu/~asuomac/diversityinit/definition.html

Chapter 12

Lennon, J., & McCartney, P. (1966, December). When I'm sixty four. The beatles online. Retrieved August 9, 2011, from http://www.the.com/pages/beatles_whenimsixtyfour.htm

New American Bible. (1970). New York: Thomas Nelson.

Obama, B. (2009, January 29). The agenda: Civil Rights. The White House. Retrieved April 22, 2009, from http://www.whitehouse.gov/agenda/civil_rights/

Back Cover

CBS News. (2011, July 27). Long-term unemployed facing discrimination? Retrieved August 10, 2011, from http://www.cbsnews.com/2102-500202_162-20084021.html?tag=contentMain;contentBody

U.S. Equal Employment Opportunity Commission. (2011, January 11). EEOC reports job bias charges hit record high of nearly 100,000 in fiscal year 2010. *EEOC Press Release.* Retrieved August 1, 2011, from http://www.eeoc.gov/eeoc/newsroom/release/1-11.11.cfm

INDEX

E

Economic Crisis ix

Economy, Nation's Economy ix, 6, 7, 21, 31, 32, 33, 38, 48, 68, 120

EEO 111

EEO RIGHTS, LAWS AND ENFORCEMENT x, 6, 8, 11, 12, 13, 14, 15, 16, 20, 23, 26, 30, 32, 38, 40, 41, 79, 99, 103, 105, 111, 112, 117, 122

Ehrmann, Max (*See Desiderata*) 10

Eighth Circuit Court of Appeals 26

Employee[s], Employee Rights ix, x, 5, 7, 8, 9, 11, 12, 13, 14, 20, 21, 23, 24, 26, 27, 29, 30, 32, 33, 37, 39, 40, 41, 43, 44, 45, 50, 56, 57, 60, 61, 63, 64, 67, 69, 72, 73, 74, 75, 76, 79, 80, 81, 82, 83, 84, 85, 86, 87, 88, 89, 90, 91, 93, 97, 99, 100, 104, 105, 106, 108, 109, 110, 111, 112, 114, 117, 118, 121

Employer negligence 90

Employers' defense 74

Employer[s'] Market x, 79

Employer[s'] negligent actions 90

Employer[s-s'] x, 2, 4, 5, 7, 8, 9, 12, 13, 20, 23, 24, 27, 30, 32, 33, 35, 37, 38, 39, 40, 41, 43, 44, 45, 48, 51, 53, 55, 56, 57, 59, 60, 61, 62, 64, 66, 74, 75, 76, 77, 78, 79, 80, 87, 88, 90, 92, 93, 97, 98, 99, 100, 103, 104, 105, 106, 107, 108, 109, 110, 113, 117

Employment At Will (EAW) 9, 13

Employment, Employment at Will Agreement x, 2, 4, 5, 6, 7, 8, 9, 11, 12, 15, 20, 21, 22, 25, 26,
27, 28, 31, 32, 35, 36, 40, 44, 45, 46, 47, 51, 52, 55, 57, 60, 61, 62, 64, 68, 71, 73, 75, 76, 79, 83, 85, 86, 87, 96, 98, 102, 103, 104, 105, 106, 107, 110, 111, 113, 116, 117, 119, 120, 121, 122, 123, 124, 127, 128

Employment Practice[s] 27, 52

ENRON 69

Epidemic ix, 29, 33, 117

Equal Credit Opportunity Act – [ECOA] 18

Equal Employment Opportunity Commission – [EEOC] x, 4, 5, 6, 8, 17, 21, 23, 26, 28, 29, 30, 32, 36, 37, 40, 41, 43, 46, 47, 48, 50, 51, 52, 53, 63, 76, 78, 90, 97, 98, 99, 100, 106, 111, 112, 114, 120, 121, 122, 123, 124, 127, 128

Equal Employment Opportunity – [EEO] x, 6, 8, 11, 12, 13, 14, 15, 16, 20, 23, 26, 30, 32, 38, 40, 41, 79, 99, 103, 105, 111, 112, 117, 122

Equality, Equal Rights, Equal Rights Laws x, 2, 4, 5, 7, 8, 9, 11, 12, 13, 15, 16, 18, 19, 20, 21, 26, 32, 33, 39, 40, 45, 46, 47, 51, 54, 59, 61, 66, 68, 70, 71, 72, 76, 77, 79, 81, 96, 97, 102, 103, 104, 105, 106, 115, 118, 120, 121, 122, 123, 124, 127, 128

Equal Pay Act [EPA], Equal Pay 15, 18, 46

Erik Paulsen Congressman Minnesota's 3rd District 5, 6

Ethan Vandersand vs. Wal-Mart Stores Inc. 96

Exposed Liability 13, 23, 81, 84

I

Idealistic 27

Illegal 21, 24, 44, 84

Illinois Care Right of Conscience Act 96

info@eeoc.gov 120

Injustice[s] x, 3, 9, 18, 20, 34, 69, 90, 101, 103, 113, 119

Intentional Discrimination 113

Interstate I 35 W, Bridge Disaster 48, 49, 50, 59, 73

Investigate, Investigative, Investigation[s], Investigating 4, 5, 19, 22, 25, 26, 27, 28, 32, 40, 43, 51, 52, 65, 70, 78, 86, 88, 89, 90, 91, 92, 93, 97, 98, 99, 100, 106, 112

Iraq, Iraqi War 37

J

Job Bias Claims 6, 32, 47, 124

Job Discrimination Claims 47

Jobless Benefits 57, 59, 60, 61, 62, 63, 64, 65, 66, 71, 102, 107

Jobless, Joblessness 2, 32, 104

Jobless Rate 60, 61

Job Losses 48

Joe Biden Vice President of the United States 119

John Carlin, Archivist of the United States, EEO 13, 122

John Lennon and Paul McCartney 115, 127

Johnson & Higgins Incorporated 29

Joint Investigation[s] 112

JPMorgan Chase, J.P. Morgan Chase & Company 36

Judge 14, 16, 26, 27, 28, 43, 53, 54, 61, 62, 63, 64, 96, 99, 101, 103, 107, 124

Judge Jeanne E. Scott 96

Judge or Jury? 124

Jury, Jury Trial 38, 53, 62, 96, 124

Justice x, 3, 5, 9, 13, 15, 16, 21, 25, 26, 28, 34, 42, 43, 51, 54, 64, 69, 72, 77, 90, 91, 95, 96, 97, 101, 106, 107, 118, 119

K

Keystone Consolidated Industries Incorporated 30

King Jr., Martin Luther x, 77, 121, 126

L

Labor Department 4, 78, 120, 126, 127

Laborer 118

Law Clerk 96

Lawrence, Wanda 77

Lee, Thomas (Annuities face-off for Swanson and Allianz. *Star Tribune*) 101

Legal, Legalize[d], Legally, Legally Disabled, Legal Liability 1, 4, 5, 12, 13, 14, 15, 18, 26, 27, 28, 34, 37, 38, 40, 45, 51, 52, 54, 62, 75, 76, 77, 78, 81, 90, 92, 95, 96, 97, 100, 101, 102, 104, 105, 106, 107, 108, 109

Legal Loop Holes 4, 12, 62, 75, 78, 96

Legal system 26, 27, 54, 76, 77, 95, 96, 104

Lehman Brothers Inc. 70, 72

Lennon, John and McCartney, Paul (*When I'm Sixty-Four*) 115, 127

Liability, liabilities 9, 13, 16, 18, 20, 23, 24, 45, 59, 80, 81, 84, 92, 102, 103, 105, 108

Litigate, Litigation 27, 33, 37, 99

M

Madoff, Bernie (Bernard L. Madoff) 72

Main Street (Main Street America) 5, 58, 71, 119

Martin Luther King Jr. x, 77, 121, 126

Matthew 16:26 27

Max Ehrmann 10

McDonnell Douglas Corporation vs. Green 74, 126

McGuire, William 72

Medicare 101

Memorial Day 2009 41

Merrill Lynch, Merrill Lynch & Company 70

Michigan Steel Tubing Company 17

Middle-Aged In America 102

Middle-Age, Middle-Aged 7, 8, 9, 12, 16, 20, 24, 28, 38, 40, 64, 75, 102, 103, 104, 105, 107, 117

Middle-East (Middle-Eastern Wars) ix, 21, 37, 111

Minneapolis, Minnesota, MPLS, MN 18, 48, 49, 73, 124

Minnesota Department of Employment and Economic Development – [DEED] 55, 56, 57, 59, 60, 61, 62, 63, 64, 65, 78, 99, 107, 114

Minnesota Department of Human Rights – [MDHR] 52, 53, 59, 114

Minnesota Department of Labor and Industry – [DOLI] 4, 5, 78, 86, 90, 91

Minnesota Department of Transportation – [MNDOT] 59

Minnesota Human Rights Act – [MHRA] 4, 5, 6, 26, 40, 63, 78, 90, 97, 99, 106

Minnesota Nice 6

Minnesota Occupational Safety and Health Act – [MNOSHA] 4, 78, 88, 90, 91, 92, 93, 94

Minnesota Office of Revisor 124, 125

Minnesota Politician[s] 33, 57, 58

Minnesota Rule 5210.0420 Subp. 2 89, 124

Minnesota Schools (2) & (5) Districts of Retired Teachers 29

Minnesota Statute 268.095, Subd. 1, Subd. 3 (a)3 63, 125

Minnesota Statute (MN) 268.095 Subdivision 1, Subdivision 3, 3 (a), 268.105 Subdivision 1, 5 (a) 63

Minnesota Statutes 363.14 (2) 53

Misconduct 60, 97, 111

Mistrust 98

Morgan Stanely & Company 70

Mortgage[s] 18, 72, 111

Mountain of Equality 19

MSNBC.com 124

N

National Americanism Commission 43

Nation's Economic Crisis ix

Native American[s] 77

Nestle Beich Incorporated 30

New American Bible – [NAB] 27, 119

New Record High 6, 32, 47, 124, 128

Nike 18, 19

No Collateral Estoppel 63

Non-Oral Hearing 64

W